Just As It Was

Best Wishes Glanis
Lyn Wilkinson

Author Name

Lyn Wilkinson – Donc UK

Hereby identified as author of this work in accordance with section 77 of the copyright design and patents act 1977

© Lyn Wilkinson 2012
ISBN 978-1-4716-2647-0

Just as it Was

Preface

Julie Spencer spent her childhood growing up in the turbulent times of the second world war. On leaving school after taking her school certificate she began her nurse training. At sixteen years old Julie was too young to go into the training school and for a while she was put straight onto the wards. She was immediately caught up in the trauma and disasters which make up life in a busy general Hospital. There was no quarter given and she was sometimes on the receiving end of the tongue of the dreaded Sister McDermott.

Her new career introduced her to people from all walks of life and the difference from her home lifestyle where her hard working parents struggled to pay the bills opened up new avenues for her. Working with her nursing colleagues wasn't always grim. The young nurses liked a bit of fun just as much as any other youngsters and their antics such as 'Where did the Vicar's organ Go?' and 'What happened to Sister Robson's Bell?' were episodes which brought relief from the sometimes sombre work.

Julie found love and romance along the way and she also found herself immersed in situations where her loyalties were sorely tested. There were difficult choices to be made and the goal was her state registration..

Just as it Was

Dedication

To my husband and love of many years. To our children and to all the generations of our families present and past who made us who we are. To friends may I say your friendship is treasured respected and enjoyed. Families and friends are the bricks from which our lives are built.

Thank you all.

Just as it Was

Disclaimer.

The author would like to point out that although the story is based upon her experiences while training at the South Yorkshire Hospital during this period, the story is fiction based on some facts. Characters names have been changed and relationships and incidents have been enhanced to add interest to the story.

Just as it Was

Straight From School

Against the gloom of an early autumn evening the street lights cast dim shadows distorting images of the local hospital over the surrounding area the year was nineteen forty seven. As people sat comfortably around their hearths in the nearby homes listening to the perfect diction of Alvar Liddel reading the nine o'clock news two young women stood waiting for the bus which would take them on the first leg of their journey home. 'Ooh my feet are killing me.' It was Julie Spencer's first day on the wards at the Royal Infirmary she was exhausted after a long shift and her new black lace up shoes were pinching her feet. Her companion Vera Sutton who was a second year nurse looked at her quizzically, sister had given her the task of taking on the youngster who had only just finished her education after taking her school certificate. 'What made you come into nursing, you're not old enough to go into training school yet?'

'I don't know really' she was silent for a moment. 'I suppose it was when someone came into school and talked about nursing as a career. There was an article in the Gazette about it as well and that made me decide, I wanted to do something useful and help people. I'd always liked the idea of being a nurse from being young and playing with dolls.'

Just as it Was

'Listen to Florence Nightingale, you're not playing with dolls now love get your feet in a bowl of hot water tonight and you'll be ready for duty again tomorrow, come on here's our bus.'

Julie hurried down the long deserted street where she lived with her parents, her two older sisters and younger brother John. The houses had been built in the late 1800s when Doncaster had developed her industries. The town had grown and flourished with the coming of the railway and the opening of the coal mines. The houses were terraced, the width of one room running through from the tiny sitting room at the front, the living room, and the small scullery at the back. The fronts of the houses were all in darkness as their occupants spent the evenings in the back living rooms. The street was lonely and ill lit. Pitch black openings of the alleyways between the houses on the opposite side of the road made her afraid. Stories sometimes circulated the neighbourhood of men lurking there and accosting young women. The labyrinthine nature of the area would provide them with an easy getaway and Julie was glad when she reached her home, eagerly lifting the knocker and rapping on the door. She heard her mother shuffle down the passageway mumbling to herself then the bolt was pulled back and the key turned in the lock. 'Where have you been?' Mrs Spencer was tight lipped as she opened the door to her daughter. 'Oh gosh I'm in for it now Julie thought, she knew how worked up her Mum could get when she was anxious.

Just as it Was

'Have you been into town?' Mrs Spencer's face was angry she spoke sharply and she glared at her daughter it was now half-past nine at night and Julie had left home at eight-o'clock that morning.

'Mum! I've had a right day' Julie was upset at being challenged, 'I've been working hard' this wasn't the homecoming that she'd expected. 'Where've you been 'til this time then?'

'I was off from two till four and I had to go to the sewing room to be measured up for some more uniform then I had to go back on duty 'til half-past eight.'

'Well it's too cold to stand in this passage talking, take your coat off.' Julie did as she was told and followed her mother into the living room. Her sister Doris was putting her hair up in dinkie curlers getting ready for bed and she had listened interestedly to what her sister had said. She had left school at fourteen and after working in service for a local business family she now worked in a factory which had made munitions during the war. Doris resented the fact that her sister had just started work at the age of sixteen and she was ready to have a go. 'You wont be able to come to the dance with us on Saturday then if this is what time you get home poor old you.'

'Don't start you two, there's no need for that.' Mr Spencer intervened. Doris paused in her hair curler task and looked towards her sister she always took her mother's side, they both felt that they were pushed into a role in life which was unfair. Their lot had been to leave school with just a very basic education at an early age and sometimes they made life

Just as it Was

hard for Julie. Babs who was the eldest had also been in domestic service. She had worked for a family in Lancashire, the husband was a G.P, and the family were generous and considerate. Later Babs had begun nurse training as a probationer at a hospital in Manchester but through ill health she had to end her training, now like her sister she worked in a local factory, Julie glared back at Doris. 'I will get some evenings off the off duty changes, sister puts it up every week.' Doris relented Julie was looking upset, 'you'll get used to it' she said.

'They're funny hours,' Dad looked at his daughter over the top of his glasses, 'you want to get a cup o'cocoa and get off to bed lass, you look done in.'

Barbara stepped in, 'go on up to the bathroom, I'll make your cocoa, you'll feel better after a good night's sleep.'

'Thanks sis, I am ready for bed.' She climbed the stairs and after a quick wash in the back bedroom which also served as the bathroom she pulled on her nightdress and cardigan then joined the family downstairs again.

'We're late tonight, look at the time it's ten o'clock.' Mrs Spencer picked up the cups and after washing them up she took them back to the living room where the table was laid for breakfast next morning. 'We've to be up at six o'clock, come on you lot.' Julie made her way upstairs calling to the family tomorrow though I've got a half-past ten off duty so I'll be able to have a lie in.'

JUST AS IT WAS

Lyn Wilkinson

Duty, Love, Laughter, Heartache.

Set in the South Yorkshire town of Doncaster in the late forties and early fifties. Julie Spencer leaves school and goes straight into nurse training at the local hospital. This young girl becomes a feisty young woman, learning from her experiences and encounters to the extent that her mother tells her:

"Remember where you come from, You're getting too big for your boots"

Price £7.49
Available from: The Tourist Information Office
"The Blue Room" 38-40 High St. Doncaster

Also available from Lulu.com:
Buy -biographies and memoirs -Lyn Wilkinson -"Just As It Was"

Just as it Was

'Nurse where have you been?' Sister Robson looked reprimandingly at Julie as she reported for duty the next day. 'I had a ten thirty off duty sister, I'm not late.'

'You don't come on at ten thirty, you go off didn't anyone explain that to you?' Julie gulped as she shook her head what a strange arrangement she thought, she was near to tears. 'You've a lot to learn, this time I'll let you off.' Sister Robson gave a little shake of her head after all the girl was only on the ward because she was too young to go into the preliminary training school until the following January. At almost seventeen she still looked like a child, 'you'll be pleased to know that Mrs Crowther in bed one has been asking where you were, you made a good impression on her yesterday, she's going home tomorrow so that she can be there for her little girl's birthday.' Julie looked pleased, she thought of the conversation that she had while cleaning Mrs Crowther's locker yesterday, she was surprised at the news of her going home because the lady didn't look well at all. She had shown Julie the photograph of an impish curly haired three year old and told her 'we thought we weren't going to have any children, we'd been married a long time when Susie was born, and it was the happiest day of our lives, she'll be three in a couple of days time.'

'Off you go, you've to change the water glasses, and you can say hello to Mrs Crowther on your way round.' With that Sister Robson followed Julie out of the office and prepared to do her daily inspection of the patients making sure that the ward was in good order with the bed corners all neatly turned and the pillowcase openings facing away from the door ready for the

Just as it Was

deputy matron to make her daily visit. Julie collected the trolley from the kitchen and made her way around the long Nightingale ward picking up the jugs and glasses as she went. She reached Mrs Crowther's bed and saw that the patient was resting but as Julie picked up her glass the woman opened her eyes and smiled. 'Hello Mrs Crowther, how are you today?'

'I'm so happy have you heard the news,? they're letting me go home for Susie's birthday tomorrow but I have to come back again for some more treatment.'

'That's lovely news, I bet you can't wait, she'll be so happy to see you, you'll be able to tell me all about it when you come back. I'm in trouble though I got my off duty wrong so I'll have to be quick with the drinks round, everybody's waiting for fresh water. I'll be looking forward to hearing about Susie's party when you get back.' She pushed the trolley on to the next patient then having finished giving out the drinks she joined the first year nurse in the sluice to help with the cleaning.

Mrs Spencer was shaking the rug in the back yard as Rosie her next-door neighbour called over the wall to her. 'How's your Julie going on? I bet she's finding it hard at the hospital.' Rosie was a Londoner who had settled in Yorkshire after marrying Tom who was noticeable mostly by his absence. How the two of them had ever got together was a mystery and something that Rosie never talked about. She had worked before her marriage as a nanny in London and her standards were very high. She seemed to support the household by

Just as it Was

taking in washing and her own home was polished, scrubbed, and fettled industriously. Now well into her sixties, wearing a wrap around pinny tied around her skinny frame she was ready to indulge in a little over the garden wall talk. Julie's mum walked up to the wall and leant on her sweeping brush as she shook her head. 'They're long hours, and funny as well, she'll take a while to get used to it.' Mrs Spencer had always run her home in a similar way to the timetables printed by the L.N.E.R the rail company for which her husband worked. The disruption to the household was upsetting her routine and the thought of having to adjust was a bit alarming for her. 'I'll give her 'til the end of the week, she's too young, and anyway what made her want to go into nursing?' Rosie waited for an answer. 'I don't know,' Mrs Spencer paused and put her hand up to her chin. 'She saw a piece in the gazette about nursing careers, they made it sound pretty exciting, I suppose that was it. She could have gone into the plant offices or teaching. She thought about that but she's been at school long enough so we didn't encourage it.' Again, the two shook their heads at the perceived strangeness of the young, then, 'I see Mr Spencer's been busy, that's a lovely blue colour, a bit bright though.'

'He's gone a bit too far I think' Julie's mum looked rather put out as she lowered her voice 'He helped old Jack Preston to do a bit of joinery and Jack gave him a couple of tins of blue paint in payment.' Her husband really had gone a bit over the top. In his enthusiasm he had painted the window frames, the outside toilet door and the back gate with the brilliant blue paint, and with some of what remained he painted the sit up and beg bicycle which Julie was going to have to use to get to work on Sundays. The girl had no other way of travelling to work and cycling through the main roads towards the hospital in her uniform on the brilliant blue bike would certainly make her unmissable to anyone else on the roads. 'Has he used it all up now?' Rosie couldn't hide her amusement.

'Not quite, I've hidden the rest though before he starts on the front of the house.' The two women laughed. 'Well I'll have to get on I've the bedrooms to finish before I start the dinner.'

'And my whites'll 'ave finished boiling' Rosie said, and with that the two women went indoors. Wait till I tell Julie her mother thought, I wonder what she'll think about that I wonder if Rosie's right.

'You're to go to first dinner' Sister Robson stopped Julie on the corridor as she was on her way to the linen cupboard to get clean sheets to put on the bed making trolley. 'Nurse Walker is on first dinner so you can go down to the dining room with her.'

'Yes sister.' Just before half-twelve the two young nurses made their way down to the dining room. They walked down the corridor passing matron's office and the sisters dining room where word had it that there was silver service and senior nursing staff were waited on by maids in black uniforms, with white headdresses. Passing this room the two approached the one at the end of the corridor from where a loud buzz of conversation flowed. About forty nurses were seated at tables each year with her own group. The staff

Just as it Was

nurses were seated together and the tables were arranged in order of seniority. Julie felt overwhelmed by the scene and the numbers and the strangeness of it all. Her companion found two seats inviting Julie to sit next to her and then immediately she launched into an animated conversation with the nurse sitting on the other side of her. Julie felt uncomfortable and isolated she didn't know a soul and wished that she were anywhere but there at that moment. 'Are you new?' a pretty blonde lively looking nurse from the opposite side of the table spoke to Julie who blushed and nodded her head. 'Are you hungry? we'll be served soon.'

'I'm not really very hungry,' Julie felt strange among all the others who seemed to know exactly who they were and what they had to do. Her appetite had deserted her.

'When did you start here I haven't seen you before?'

'Only yesterday I'm on ward three I'm going into P.T.S. in January.'

'I've been out of P.T.S. for six months now, do you live in?'

'No I live in Wysten, it's not far away, but I'll have to live in when I go into school.'

'You will, I think you'll like it though.' As Julie picked up her plate with the meat pie and vegetables on it which she had been given sitting at the table full of strangers she wasn't too sure about that.

Reporting back on duty the next hour was spent tidying the beds and getting the patients and the ward ready for visiting

Just as it Was

time. A screen was drawn across the double glass entrance doors until promptly at two-o'clock the screen was drawn back and visitors carrying flowers and bottles of cordial and clean nightwear flooded onto the ward. The three nurses who were on duty gathered in the sterilizer room to fill the drums with cotton wool and gauze swabs after which they were ready to go down to the large steriliser and be brought back up to the ward to be used on the dressing trolley. It was an opportunity for the nurses to talk as they worked and they kept a vigilant eye on things through the glass porthole in the heavy sluice door. Third year nurse Brenda Guy was a short heavily built girl with a stern expression and thick dark hair, which was cut severely short. This afternoon she was in charge, any problems and staff nurse from the male ward on the adjoining floor would be consulted. 'The ward's quiet at the moment' she said. Indeed most of the patients were recovering from surgery and beds had been kept empty to accommodate any urgencies, which might have to be admitted. 'Fingers crossed though it can alter quite quickly.' Completing their task Guy turned to Julie, 'Spencer' she said, Julie had quickly become used to being addressed by her surname, 'would you take these raffle tickets around the visitors, you being young and pretty they're more likely to buy from you.'

'What are they for?' Julie wasn't too keen on the idea and she wasn't taken in by the manipulative compliment either. 'The Hospital Funds Committee need extra cash for items on the ward. We used to go out with collecting tins but now we try to raise a bit of money on visiting days with raffles.'

Just as it Was

'I never expected having to do this' but with a deep sigh and picking up the tickets the young nurse took an intake of breath and set off around the ward smilingly greeted on the whole by the visitors who dug into their purses and their pockets. There was one urgency during the afternoon, a lady who had fallen from her bicycle and received cuts and abrasions. When asked she told nurse Guy and Nurse Spencer that her name was Jenny Maria Blunt she was to be bed-bathed and kept in overnight because of her concussion. After visiting time the ward routine ran smoothly as the senior staff did the pulse and temperature round and gave out the medication, Julie and Vera did the bedpan round after supper and tidied up the patient's lockers. Mrs Crowther was sleepy as Julie approached 'Wont be long now' she whispered 'I'll see you tomorrow.'

'Have you been busy today? Mrs Spencer was putting out biscuits and a bedtime drink for the family as Julie arrived home. 'Busy enough Mum my feet still ache those wards are really long fifteen beds down each side.'

'You'll have to get a pair of roller skates' Doris laughed. 'Anyway you've a half day off tomorrow haven't you so you'll be able to come to the dance with us after all.'

Just as it Was

2

Colin

The morning was spent routinely cleaning lockers and collecting the water glasses and jugs and generally helping the junior nurse with the bed-pan round. Some of the patients were to be discharged leaving empty beds in case of more urgencies. Julie was surprised at how quickly she was getting used to the routine and she looked forward to the time when she would go into school to learn some of the procedures. She was allowed to watch but she longed for the time when she could be more involved. After going back up to the ward having been in to first dinner she reported off duty and in her black stockings and shoes and navy blue silk head-wear and gabardine she headed for the bus stop. What will I do with my half day? she asked herself as she caught the bus home. Doris and Babs had gone into town to do some shopping and Mum was preparing the Sunday lunch so that tomorrow she could take things a bit easier. The small living room was overheated by the glowing fire which warmed the side-oven where the Sunday roast was well on it's way to being cooked. There would only be the Yorkshire Puds to make and the vegetables to cook, and Mum could enjoy a long lazy afternoon. Julie's parents usually spent Sunday afternoon sitting around the fire chatting and nodding off and sometimes a friend or relative might pop in. At teatime out would come the salad, the salmon and the trifle it was all a bit routine and predictable. Sometimes as the youngsters sat around the fire and spotted a stranger on the bars of the fire grate they enlivened the dull hours by guessing who it might be that would be visiting. As a growing girl Julie had often longed for someone exciting to knock on the door and liven things up. If only one of those smashing looking lads who she sometimes went to watch at the towns football matches was to make an unexpected visit. How exciting would that be!

'Oh by the way I was talking to Mrs Thompson about you.'

'What were you saying Mum?'

'She was asking me how you're getting on, she doesn't think you'll stick it at the hospital.' Julie Spencer looked pointedly towards her mother. 'Why did she say that, course I'll stick it' the remark made her even more determined to go through with her nursing career. 'Tell her she's wrong Mum, I'll stick it.' After changing into a skirt and blouse Julie decided to take Sherry out for a walk. 'I could do with a bit of fresh air' she told her mum. Putting on a warm jacket she put the dog on her lead and walked over the bridge to the nearby park. As she left behind the rows of terraced houses and the streets she relaxed and enjoyed the freedom of the open space Julie loved the outdoors. As the light breeze tousled her hair she walked on reaching the Flatts she looked forward to walking over the soft lush grass, such a contrast to the hard wooden floors of the hospital. The bronzed autumn light shone through the treetops dappling the roof and the walls of the cafe. People wandered in and out for drinks and one of the

Just as it Was

famed little cheesecakes which were supplied by the local bakery. She imagined the pleasure of times when she had bought them. A mixture of light puff pastry and milk curds they were a favourite of hers but today Julie resisted the temptation and walked on with the dog. A movement caught her eye as a playful breeze caused her to turn her head and she delighted in the swaying of the trees and the flight of the last swallows as they glided towards the eaves of the old boathouse. Letting Sherry off the lead the dog scampered off and then rolled onto her back revelling in the exercise. Julie chuckled to herself as she watched all of this wishing that she could live in the countryside. It was a dream of hers since childhood to live where she could awake to the sight of fields and trees and little brooks ever since her brief holidays on her Uncle's smallholding on the edges of Yorkshire and Lancashire where she had learned to love the sight of the old stone walls and the vast panoramas of the skies. She disliked intensely the monotonous rows of houses with their smoking chimneys the never ending unwieldy pavements and the grey landscape with hardly a tree or a blade of grass in sight when she opened the doors of her home. There were few people about as she moved into the park's playground. One or two small children were being pushed on the swings by their parents. Walking on towards the tennis courts she saw that they were deserted and thoughts of the school holidays when she had played there with her friends ran through her mind. Where were they all now? life had changed so much since she had started work at the hospital. Her old friends were starting out in their careers as she was, some had gone on to college and

Just as it Was

university, others were employed in and around Doncaster many of them in offices. There was little opportunity for her to see them with the irregular hours that she was on duty. The secure friendships of school-days were mostly gone and a new life was opening up before her. In this reflective mood she decided to take the path down by the river Don which flowed through the park. The path was deserted and as she walked along the river bank Julie's attention was caught by the branches from the bushes which overhung the water as they trailed and floated gently sweeping over the flotsam which had gathered on the surface of the river. The rotting smell of decaying foliage was a familiar reminder of outings taken previously accompanied by her family on warm September days. As children the family had all walked here together Dad had often warned them to keep away from the edge of the banking because of the danger of the bankt crumbling. She could hear her father in her mind's eye now. 'Stop that John' as her brother ventured too near to the edge. 'Somebody fell in there last week' it was enough to bring his son back to his Dad's side quick sharp. Now it was just her and Sherry. Giving herself a shake she brought herself back to the present and as she cut through the banking and back into the park she realised that the afternoon was coming to a close. Out into the streets again Julie saw that a few shoppers were making their way home carrying baskets and bags after doing the week-end shopping. The town was proud of it's excellent indoor fish and butchers' market and stall-holders on the outside market sold fresh vegetables and fruit. Doris and Babs would probably have returned home by now with fresh

Just as it Was

food for the family which their mother had asked them to bring. The fish and chip shop would soon be open she noticed as she saw the Newbys preparing to start cooking for their teatime trade. It would be ham hock, with freshly baked bread and home made pickles at their house tonight, followed by a selection of cakes and pastries baked by her mother yesterday to keep them supplied through the week.

'I wonder what time Steve will get here, he's bringing Eric?' Doris stood in front of the mirror, which hung over the fireplace putting the last touches to her make up. 'Don't put too much of that lipstick on' her Dad told her as he shook his newspaper out before turning the page. He was sitting in his armchair reading the evening paper and smoking his pipe after he had listened to the football results on the wireless. The family had eaten and he was now surrounded by the girls who were getting ready for their evening out. He was very aware off his fatherly duties as he saw them, the responsibility of three unmarried daughters was something to be considered he felt. Since the war the effect that those

G. Is. had on girls had changed things, not that his girls had anything to do with them but the world was a different place now. 'And don't get too near that fire' the Spencer's living room was lit from one central light bulb and in order for any of them to see into the mirror to check out their hair and make-up, the only place for the mirror to be of any use was over the fireplace. They were almost ready now and the last time that Julie had gone to the church hall dance with her sisters she had met a good looking lad of about seventeen, he was a

Just as it Was

good dancer and she hoped that she would see him there again. 'Do you like my dress? I got it from Bon Marche it was only fifteen shillings.' Doris looked at her sister and admired the frock with it's nipped in waist and full skirt. 'I bet you're hoping that lad'l be there again the one you were dancing with last time.'

'I'm not, that's not why I bought it.'

'Well it looks very nice.' Babs said. There was a knock on the door, 'here they are now.' Steve and Doris had met during the war when he was in the air force and stationed at nearby Finningley he often caught the bus from his small home-town to see her and take her out to the pictures or dancing. She answered the door and seconds later a youth appeared on his own in the living room. 'Where's Doris?' Dad looked for his daughter as shouts of 'coming' were mingled with whispered endearments being exchanged in the passageway. Moments later Steve came through into the living room accompanied by his fiancée, the young man was still standing just within the room looking awkward as Steve introduced him. 'This is Eric.'

Although older he looked about sixteen and he shuffled and looked nervous as he held out his hand. 'Hello' he squeaked, his voice had hardly broken. He wasn't bad looking and Julie wondered if he'd been brought along especially for her I'm not being paired up with him, I really do hope Colin'll be there tonight, she thought.

Just as it Was

The church hall was a rather dismal looking place dark green paint peeling woodwork and a badly lit toilet were it's main features but it served the community well. Whist drives and jumble sales and scout and guide evenings were held there regularly and a youth club had recently been set up. The hall was hardly conducive to glamour with notices abounding giving the dates of the weekly meeting of the Mothers Union and advertisements for the services of the local chiropodist prominently displayed. Julie longed for romance but it was hard to imagine the possibility of a romantic encounter as in the sumptuous Hollywood settings of Fred Astaire and Ginger Rogers. They met and fell in love in silken draped ballrooms decorated by huge arrangements of exotic flowers on pedestals and the accompaniment of trombones, trumpets, and a whole army of musical instruments. The church hall would have to suffice. She looked around, no sign of Colin but she hadn't given up hope yet. Glamour may not have reached Wysten but the girls were pretty the men were bold and they liked to dance and they were determined to enjoy themselves. As the duo struck up 'Put Your Arms Around Me Baby' a tune from a recent film Eric turned to her 'shall we have a go?' In the absence of other requests Julie joined him on the small dancing area. 'Is it a waltz, I can only do waltzes.'

'Just look at my feet and hold on tight, it's a quickstep' she said.

It wasn't bad last night. Julie awoke with remnants of the evening out uppermost in her mind. She had danced several times with Eric and Steve who was an excellent dancer had

Just as it Was

twirled her expertly around the floor as Doris looked on approvingly. Colin hadn't turned up and that was a disappointment but now it was Sunday morning and she had to make her way to the hospital on the much maligned bright blue sit up and beg bike. The good thing was that there weren't many onlookers so early on a Sunday morning; the roads were clear as she made her way to work. The five-mile journey along the quiet roads was pleasant; her navy head veil flew out behind her and a group of Irish road workers shouted cheerily to her as she battled against the breeze. She responded with a wave and a smile and soon she arrived safely and on time at the hospital. Putting the bike out of sight in a corner of the bike shed she walked along to the cloakroom and changed out of her outdoor uniform putting on her cap and apron she then made her way up to the ward. Walking along the corridor leading onto the female ward Staff Nurse Brown caught her up. 'Did you have a nice half-day?'

'Yes thanks, oh!' Julie almost fell over a mattress, which was propped up against the wall; her attention had been distracted as she had turned to speak to her companion.

'What's that doing there?'

'It's waiting to be taken down to the sterilisation room by one of the porters. Julie it's from Mrs Crowther's bed.'

'Why, she's coming back isn't she?' Staff Nurse Brown looked at Julie and spoke quietly.

'There's no easy way to tell you this, I know how you chatted to Mrs Crowther about her little girl; Julie I'm afraid' she hesitated then looking at Julie said 'I'm afraid that Mrs

Just as it Was

Crowther died on the ward as she was getting ready to go home.'

'No!' it was too cruel. Julie cried out, she was stunned. The older nurse put her arms around the girl as she collapsed in a flood of tears.'Come into the office' Staff Brown led Julie into sister's office 'sit down Nurse' she said gently. She gave the young girl a minute or two to compose herself then she said to her 'one of the worst things about nursing is that we sometimes see people die. It's pretty rare and naturally we get upset when it happens, if we didn't we'd be poor nurses, caring is why we come into this profession. Mrs Crowther was desperately ill and it was a compassionate decision to let her go home for her little girls birthday. Unfortunately she had a heart attack and died as she was preparing to go home, one of those things, which no one could have foreseen.'

'So she didn't even get home to see her little girl?'

Staff nurse shook her head as Julie looked towards her. 'Now Nurse Spencer this is a dreadful thing that has happened right at the start of your working on this ward but we have to cope with such things. Take a few minutes, dry your eyes, and then you can go onto the ward, you have patients who need your help.'

Disaster

Julie pushed the trolley around the ward as she tidied and wiped down the lockers. Sister Robson was there giving out the post and chatting to the patients as she went; she handed out letters and a few get well cards which always put a smile on the recipients faces. Sister also watched the young nurse as she collected the water jugs and glasses and spoke easily, sometimes having a bit of fun with the patients. She's settled in quite well, very conscientious and friendly sister noticed. Julie took the trolley into the kitchen for the empty jugs and glasses to be washed by the cleaners. After that she did the bedpan round. It was time for the assistant matron's inspection of the ward which was looking s pick and span as the stern looking Miss Mc Dermot went to the foot of each bed and asked 'Good morning how are you' to which each patient responded with 'I'm alright thank you matron' and with that she moved swiftly on her eyes all over the place, Julie could never understand why they all said that they were alright they wouldn't be in hospital if they were all right, would they? Completing her round of the ward Miss Mc Dermot went into the sluice to inspect that area. 'Sister' she asked, 'who is your junior?' Sister Robson smiled pleasantly, anticipating compliments. 'It's Julie Spencer a very young nurse, she hasn't been into P.T.S. yet.'

'Please ask Nurse Spencer to come here and speak to me.' In her plain navy blue dress and frilly cap the assistant matron was a forbidding figure, Julie approached her nervously. 'Oh nurse, good morning, I understand that you have cleaned the lockers this morning.'

'Yes matron,' what was this all about, Julie didn't know what to think.

'Is this one ready to go back onto the ward?'

'It is Matron' Miss Mc Dermot took out her pencil and with the sharp point she poked into the corner of the locker. 'Look at that nurse,' there was a very small piece of black fluff simply minute on the end of the pencil. Looking directly at Julie she said sternly 'all that you do nurse, do with your might, things done by half, are never done right.'

'Please Miss McDermott there are hardly any bristles left on my scrubbing brush.'

'I don't want excuses nurse, remember what I said.' With that the assistant matron walked out of the sluice followed by a dismayed Sister Robson. Well I thought I was going to get a bit of praise, after all that washing and polishing I can't believe that I've just been told off. The perceived injustice built up resentment in Julie and for two pins she would have answered Miss McDermott back given half the chance. Instead tears began to well in her eyes. Sister Robson came back into the sluice she had been amazed at the criticism from Miss Mc Dermott and she thought it best to give the girl something

Just as it Was

else to do, she realised how near to tears Julie was. 'Nurse, will you find a doctor and get him to sign this drug request for me.' She thought that the best thing was to get her off the ward for a while. When ordering replacement drugs for the ward's stock cupboard a doctor's signature was necessary and a search went out if the houseman wasn't about. 'I should try casualty first you should find someone there.' Julie took the form from sister and hurried on her way. She was quite angry now as she made her way down to the ground floor feeling quite upset and disgruntled. Totally absorbed in her thoughts she entered the swing doors into the casualty area with some force and the next minute she tripped and bumped into a young man wearing a white coat and with a stethoscope hung around his neck. She almost fell but a pair of strong arms held her and she looked up into a pair of merry brown eyes topped by a thatch of lustrous thick brownish wavy hair. 'Are you O.K.?'

'Sorry, I was a bit careless, I shouldn't have pushed the door so hard.'

'Just one of those things, we were both trying to go through it from opposite sides are you sure you're O.K. it wasn't your fault don't look so upset.' The young man looked at the very pretty young nurse whom he hadn't seen around his work area before.

'I'm alright really it was my fault.'

He smiled, the most amazing smile which was just what Julie needed at the moment.

'Are you going into casualty, do you work in this department?'

Just as it Was

'No I'm on the wards, I've come to ask a doctor to sign this drug request, sister said that I would find someone down here.'

'I'll do that for you.' The young man took out his pen and quickly signed the request.

Julie looked at the signature; Dr J. Gibson, 'I'm sorry to have been a nuisance' she looked at him shyly.'

'Any-time.' the young man smiled.

'Thank you' she said and they went their separate ways. Back on the ward Mrs Bolton who was two days post- op called Julie over. 'Can I eat an apple?'she asked, picking one up from the plate, which was on the bedside locker.

'I don't know.'

' You should know you're a nurse aren't you?'

'Not yet Mrs Bolton, I've got to do my training first, I'll go and ask staff nurse if you can eat an apple.' Just a few weeks ago she had been a schoolgirl but now when the patients questioned her about what they could eat, when they could go home, if they could get out of bed they expected her to have the answers. She approached the harassed looking staff nurse, 'can Mrs Bolton eat an apple staff?'

'Yes if she's had her bowels open although it's unlikely so soon, run along and tell her, and come straight back to me, as a matter of fact we've got our hands full. We've had an alert from casualty to say that there's been a train crash I was just about to get the staff together to tell everyone, we have to prepare as many beds as we can for admissions.' Julie froze

Just as it Was

as the words sank in. 'Don't stand there Nurse Spencer tell Mrs Bolton about the apple and then come and help with the beds.'

'Shall I load up the trolley from the linen cupboard?' A train crash!' Where! How! What' would she be expected to do? A major incident to be involved in and she'd only just learnt how to cope with bedpans and giving out the drinks she knew nothing about disasters it was a word that she'd only read about in news papers and a feeling of unreality overwhelmed her. 'Go on Nurse Spencer give Mrs Bolton the news about her apple and then fetch the bed linen. As though in a dream she hurried off with her heart racing. Extra staff appeared from nowhere, off duty nurses were called in from the nurse's home and on hearing about the train crash others who lived out came in from the surrounding area. News had travelled fast medical staff were all put on alert and the theatres and casualty were set up ready for when the first ambulances arrived. Apparently two passenger trains had collided one running into the back of the other many people had died and there were many injured. 'The senior staff can deal with the badly injured; all non-essential procedures will have to be shelved. The junior staff will be left to cope with the ordinary ward routine.' A directive came from the hospital chairman of the board after hasty consultation with senior members of the medical and the nursing staff. 'We'll set up transfusion services in outpatients the two theatres will be set up and if necessary we will have surgical teams ready to work through the night.'

'What sort of injuries are we dealing with?'

Just as it Was

'Fractures, lacerations, loss of blood, there'll be internal injuries head and facial injuries as well, God knows what! we'll have to be prepared for anything. A lot of the patients will be badly shocked and of course we have relatives and friends wanting information about the injured, we must make preparations to deal with them.' The senior surgeon Ian Winstanley addressed the assembled staff. 'Here we go' the first ambulances were arriving, bells ringing urgently and the long session began.

'Nurse, I don't know where my daughter is.' A middle-aged woman who was sitting in the outpatients' hall in a wheelchair called out to Julie. She was very distressed and surrounded by patients on trolleys and people who were wandering about searching for their loved ones, as she asked for help. 'My husband's waiting to be treated by the doctor, we haven't seen our daughter since we were put into the ambulance after the crash, no-one knows anything' the woman was shaking, pleading with Julie. 'What's your name?' Julie gently took the woman's hand and bent over her, she had found an inner strength from somewhere something that she hadn't known that she possessed until now. Everyone around her was attending to peoples needs and there was plenty of demand no room for thinking about anything but helping these people who had set out on a journey this morning only to end up here in a hospital department some of them not knowing what had happened to their loved ones. 'Rolands, my name's Mrs Rolands and my daughter's name's Jane.' She spoke with a pronounced cockney accent and as Julie bent over her she burst into tears Julie handed her a paper hanky. 'Would you

Just as it Was

like me to ask if you can have a cup of tea?' the young nurse put her arms around the woman, 'and then I'll see what I can find out about Jane.' Mrs Rolands nodded her head as Julie went off to find the sister of the outpatient department where she had been sent to help out. The area was thronged with people and equipment but at last Julie found Sister Burton. 'You need to go to the records office nurse, they're doing their best to keep track of everyone, and yes Mrs Rolands can have a cup of tea, put sugar in it she's pretty shocked, I saw her not long ago and I was trying to find someone to look after her, thank goodness you arrived we need all the hands we can get down here.' Julie made her way back to Mrs Rolands with the hot sweet tea and after assuring her that she would do her best to find out about Jane she stayed and tried to comfort her. 'Can you find my husband?' tearfully Mrs Rolands looked anxiously at Julie, 'they took him down that corridor across there.'

'Yes of course I'll go and see what I can find out.' she looked hesitantly at the woman before asking quietly 'do you remember what happened to you all in the crash?' Mrs Rolands took a deep breath and dabbed her eyes before speaking. 'It's all mixed up in my mind but we were in the first train; it was slowing down when there was an almighty bang. At first everyone was shocked, glass shattered, wood splintered and there was a horrible grinding sound of metal on metal. We were thrown forward into the aisles, people were on top of one another and when we looked for Jane we couldn't find her.' She sobbed she couldn't control herself and her head dropped into her hands as she was unable to go on.

Just as it Was

Julie stood there comforting her before asking, 'can you remember what happened next?' Mrs Rolands looked up at the nurse through tear-stained eyes a strangled sob escaped as she struggled to speak. 'It was as though time stood still for a few minutes, then people were screaming and calling out to each other and then the rescuers arrived. We were taken out of the carriage and put into the ambulance. We asked about Jane, we kept calling out for her and asking people but couldn't find anything out about her.' Mrs Rolands broke out into uncontrollable sobbing. 'Oh nurse, where's my daughter?' Julie hugged the woman again telling her that she would do her best to find out and then she made her way towards the records office. 'We don't have anyone of that name on our list.' Mr Daniels who had run the records department very efficiently for many years searched through his list of names as Julie waited after asking him about Jane. 'People are still being brought in by ambulance, tell Mrs Rolands we'll let her know if there's any news. They're still bringing people out, there are so many involved.' The trauma of the tragedy was etched on his face as it was on so many others in the outpatients' hall which had been turned into the casualty reception area. Through the mass of people Julie made her way back to Mrs Rolands and gave her the news, which was no news at all really. 'I'll see if I can find your husband, perhaps this lady will stay with you while I go and look for him.' The less injured were doing what they could to help those worse off than themselves and the pert little woman who had offered to keep on eye on Mrs Rolands said 'I fought we'd done wiv all o' this when wi beat them bleedin' jerries, c'mon gal, don't give up , they'll find your daughter.' As Julie reached the corridor to which Mrs Rolands had pointed she found that it was lined with staff and patients and approaching her was a chap who was bandaged heavily around his neck and shoulder. 'You wouldn't be Mr Rolands by any chance?'

'That's me, have you any news of Jane?'

'Not yet but your wife asked me to find you come on you can have a cup of tea now that you've got your dressings done, we'll go back to her and I'll find out if there's any news of Jane how old is she by the way?'

'Sixteen, she's sixteen.' Mr Rolands struggled to stifle a sob.

'Just the same age as me' Julie thought. As patients were now being admitted to the wards from theatre and from casualty Julie was sent back to help with the ward routine. Six hours had elapsed since the first ambulance had arrived and still they came. 'Gosh I'm about done in' Vera; Nurse Sutton, greeted Julie as she returned to the ward. 'The orthopaedic wards are full and we're taking their overflow, I've to go down to theatre to bring a patient up to the ward, a young girl whose had an amputation. We've just got the bed ready and I've had to run all over to find a bed cage, we're running out of equipment.'

'Do you know her name?'

'Yes it's Jane Rolands.'

Julie had caught the last bus home, along with a scattering of young people who had been to the Saturday night dance at

Just as it Was

the Co-op. Some of the older passengers were talking to each other about the train crash, which had devastated the town. 'Hello Julie' she looked up to see a neighbour Mrs Green preparing to take the seat next to her 'you look done in.'

'I'll be glad to get home, it's been quite a day, a horrible one.'

'I 'eard about the train crash and saw ambulances rushing along ' main roads, Reg went t' bridge to see what wor going on. People from houses nearby were tekin' blankets out an' anythin' that they could lay their hands on to 'elp. They opened th'r 'ouses up to people who could walk and dipped into th'r tea and sugar rations and some of 'em even tried to give a bit o' first aid. Ooh look yer' can see' track from 'ere, th'r still workin' on it.' Julie could see the wrecked carriages and the cranes, illuminated by the floodlights. Her thoughts went back to the hospital where the theatres were still working full out. Most of all she thought of Jane Rolands and her parents who were sitting by the bedside waiting for their daughter to recover from the surgery. It was just after eleven o'clock when Julie arrived home. 'Yer Mam's gone to bed, I said I'd wait up for yer. I bet yer done in aren't yer lass?'

'I am Dad, it's been awful. I don't want to talk about it, I want to go to bed, I'm back on duty again at half past eight tomorrow.'

'Come on then, drink this cocoa then off yer go.'

The hospital was overflowing with patients who had been admitted from the crash as Julie reported on duty the next morning There were beds down the centre of the wards and

Just as it Was

the side wards were all full. As many patients as it was possible to discharge had been sent home to the care of the community physicians and nurses. The night staff wearily gave their reports. They had little respite in the twelve hours that they had been on duty, patients had been prepared for theatre and others were coming back after surgery. Pain relief had to be administered and the shocked and injured had to be consoled and eased. There had been no let-up for anyone and it looked as though the situation would remain the same for some time yet. She found Mr and Mrs Rolands still sitting by their daughter's bed. Jane looked pale and the dark smudges under her eyes told of her ordeal intravenous fluids were hung on the pole attached to the bed head and she was deeply unaware. 'Hello nurse' Mrs Rolands turned her weak smile on Julie 'I wondered if we would see you again.'

'Have you had any sleep?'

'We've nodded off a bit and the night staff said that we could go into the visitors room but we wanted to stay by Jane's bedside.'

'How is she?'

'The doctor says that she'll survive. She was trapped in the carriage by the metal supports and she was unconscious, no one knew her name.' Mrs Rolands started to cry 'I was so pleased when we found out that she was still alive.' Her lip quivered 'you know that she's had her leg off nurse.' Julie nodded, she couldn't speak, she held out her arms and the older woman moved towards her and they clung together as Mr Rolands looked on with tears in his eyes.

Just as it Was

Slowly Jane's condition improved, her parents found very reasonably priced lodgings near to the hospital and they were able to spend as much time as they wished on the ward with her. The casualties of the train crash were discharged as they recovered and Mr Winstanly was making his round accompanied by his entourage, the R.S.O. the houseman and sister and he stopped at the foot of Jane's bed. 'Now then young lady, and how are you today?'

'I want to go home.'

'You want to leave us do you, well I can't blame you for wanting to get back home,' turning to Sister Robson he asked 'Sister is the wound healed?'

'It is sir, there has been no problem with that.'

'Then in that case, I don't know why I can't discharge you to the care of your G.P. he will arrange for your treatment to continue in London. I'm sure that they'll have you walking again quite soon.' Mr Rolands held out his hand to shake that of the surgeon 'thank you sir we want to thank you and the rest of the staff for all that you have done for our daughter. The hospital and the people of this town will be remembered by us forever.'

'Good man, good man, I'll write to the necessary authority good luck in the future to you and your family Mr Rolands.' Mr Winstanley moved on to the next bed.

'So we're going to lose you? the ward had resumed it's previous routine and Julie was polishing Jane's locker. The two of them had struck up a warm friendship over the weeks.

Just as it Was

'I don't want to lose touch with you, will you write to me?' Jane asked.

'Of course I will I'll give you my address and when you're settled in at home you can drop me a line.'

'Have you ever been to London?'

'Only once when I was about ten years old. Dad took me and Mum and John. It was lovely, we went to the palace,' she laughed, 'only to stand and look of course, we weren't invited in for tea. We went to a Lyon's Corner House to eat and then we saw the Crown Jewels and Tower Bridge it was really great.'

'Will you come and see me? you can stay with us.'

'Just let me know when, but get yourself sorted out first, of course I'll come we'll paint the town red we'll make up for all this.'

Just as it Was

4

Birthday Surprise, and Mrs Keogh

'Happy birthday.' Staff Nurse Brown smiled and pushed a small gift-wrapped parcel into Julie's hands as they were putting on their caps and aprons in the little stock room before going on duty. 'How did you know?'

'We have our ways and means' the staff nurse smiled. Since working on the ward Julie had got on well with the rest of the staff but she hadn't expected them to recognise her birthday and as she opened the wrapping paper she saw that it contained a couple of items and she exclaimed as she opened them up. 'Oh, these are lovely, lipstick, just the right colour as well, and this scarf, I love it.' Julie took the Max Factor lipstick and the pretty floral chiffon scarf out of the wrapping paper and put them into her bag. She opened the birthday card which had been signed by all the staff on the ward and she was overcome by the gesture. 'I don't know what to say, I didn't expect this, thank you, it's such a lovely surprise.'

'We thought you'd go for Autumn shades, end of August birthday and your colouring.'

'Autumn's my favourite time of the year.'

'And mine but come on we can't dilly-dally it's half-past eight.'

Just as it Was

Julie was really touched by the gift from the other nurses and later she thanked them as they gathered in the kitchen at lunchtime ready to serve out the patients' meals. The kitchen was set up to keep lunch piping hot for the patients. The food had been taken from the trolley which was brought up by Jim the porter and placed in and on top of the huge hot plate and warming cabinet. As each nurse took a tray Sister Robson stood there with the stainless steel food containers in front of her serving patients in the order of the bed that they were in. 'What do you think Mrs Evans could manage today?' she was recovering from a partial gastrectomy to remove a gastric ulcer and after a regime of first thirty millilitres of sterile water and later citrated milk she was now gradually being introduced to solid food. 'Shall we try her with a little of this steamed fish?' A small amount with a very small helping of creamy mashed potato was carefully arranged on the plate. Sister continued with her task of suiting each patient individually. 'Help Mrs Dobson to get her dinner nurse, she's not feeling too well today.' It was quite a ritual and each meal was chosen thoughtfully before being taken to the patient's bedside where nurse helped them to sit up if necessary and spoon-fed them if required. It was a time for spending and forming a closeness with the patient and getting to know what they were feeling and what their thoughts were. Afterwards when everyone was served and the dinner plates collected the sweet was given out and then the used plates were collected on a trolley and taken back to the kitchen where Mrs Giddings and Mrs Keogh the two cleaning ladies washed them all up in the huge deep sink. 'Happy birthday Nurse Spencer' Mrs

Just as it Was

Keogh smiled at Julie then continued her task. She was a heart warming Scottish woman and she regaled the staff from time to time with stories of her mishaps and adventures. Today as she worked away washing up as the nurses emptied the contents of the trolleys onto the sink she talked about her latest exploit.' I nearly didna get here today,' she told them as she scraped the left over food from the plates into the food bin, her ample bosoms wobbling as she lent over She straightened up and gave a heavy sigh the nurses knew that they were in for a treat, her stories were legend. 'A wuz tekin' a short cut close to the cattle market pedalling along on ma bike nice and steady like when I heard the sound o' hoofs behind ma. I couldna believe ma ears I looked over ma shoulder to see a big black beastie just a few yards away. He was bearin' doon on ma snortin and gallopin' and I thought ma end had come. Ooo, I was fair scared to deeath, I rode like the clappers puffin' and pantin' and shoutin' for help.' The nurses were creased up with laughter, Mrs Keogh was short and stout and given to hot flushes, not the athletic type. The laughter encouraged her and she responded, 'I was sweatin' like mad and breathless he'd nearly caught up with ma when suddenly there was a shout I saw two men in front of ma with a cattle truck, the gate was doon at the back and I nearly drove into it I wuz desperate and there was hardly room to pass. Goo, on missus the men were shoutin at ma' and wavin' their arms and sticks urging ma to get by pointin' to the little space between the van and the wall at the side of it. I tell yer I wished I wuz a wee bit thinner just then. I thought I wouldna make it but I managed it, I squeezed through like

Just as it Was

toothpaste out of a tube it nearly took ma skin off. Ooh ma heart wor beatin' twenty to the dozen but I pedalled away like a rocket as fast as I could. The beastie must 'ave run into the truck, I'm surprised he didna come straight through, I think that he'd tekin' a fancy to me a'right.' Her audience couldn't stop laughing, and even her workmate Mrs Giddings managed a smile as she wiped the mountain of clean plates with her tea towel. In contrast to Mrs Keogh she was tall skinny and a bit dour and she always wore a scarf tied around her head like a turban. When standing side by side they looked like a comedy duo but they were as different as chalk and cheese. The two women worked well together however and on hands and knees every morning Mrs Giddings scrubbed the rubberised tiles on the long corridors and together with her partner took great pride in keeping the unit spotless. 'Well that was fun, what's next?' kitchen duties were finished and Vera turned to Julie. 'We're on first lunch today come on.' They walked towards the lift which would take them down to the ground floor, 'seventeen eh, you'll be in P.T.S after Christmas, you'll be able to tell sister tutor a thing or two about what you've learnt up here on the ward, don't tell her everything though' Julie laughed 'what's she like?'

'Oh she's an ogre, thinks all nurses should be toffee nosed spinsters, she's one of the old school. Don't worry about that though we all have to put up with it and we survive. A few of us are going to the Fairgrove on Saturday night after duty would you like to come with us?'

'Thanks for asking me, it's a bit late though going after duty.'

Just as it Was

'Your seventeen now Nurse Spencer, time you lived a little.' Julie wasn't sure how it would be received at home but she felt that perhaps Vera Sutton was right. 'I'll let you know' she said.

When Julie arrived home she found her mum talking with the rest of the family about a proposed visit from her Aunt and Uncle. 'I've had a letter from Uncle Harry and Auntie Freda,' she told Julie as she put her in the picture they want to visit next week and they're expecting us to put them up. It's race week, and they want a bit of a holiday.'

'It'll be a tight squeeze Mum, where are they going to sleep?'

'I've had a word with Mrs Thompson, she says that you girls can go and sleep round there so your Auntie and Uncle can have your room.'

'It's alright with me Mum.' Julie was fond of her aunt and uncle, they were from her parent's home county of Lancashire and as a child she had enjoyed holidays on their run down farm on the edge of Saddleworth Moor. Uncle Harry was a huge red-faced jovial character and along with his mongrel dog 'Terry' he had taken Julie walking on the moors and she had revelled in the open countryside and the fresh air and when she returned to the back streets of her home town again it took a while for her to settle down. Harry's ebullient nature was in contrast to her own parents sometimes constrained attitude and although he sometimes caused a few ructions, life was never dull when he was around.

Just as it Was

5

Race Week

Eva Spencer was looking out onto her small backyard through the kitchen window as she wiped down the draining board. Most of the area had been taken up with the bike shed but Eva had struggled to establish a bit of a garden and in one of the small borders she had planted London Pride and wallflowers. There was a larger area in front of the window and she was trying to get chrysanthemums to strike off in this patch with little success. Eva strived to make the best of things always and it was her ambition to make herself a decent little garden out of the small patch. She was pleased with her achievement and looked forward to showing it off. She was waiting for the arrival of her brother and his second wife all was ready for them the covers had been changed on the cushions and on the plant stand and on the small table in the front room, on which the aspidestra stood. All had been polished along with the rest of the furniture and the the smell of cleanliness and endeavour wafted through the house. The cake tins had been filled with buns and tarts made by Eva with help from Doris, and hopefully they would last the week, until the next baking day. Now all that Eva Spencer had to do was wait. The table was set ready for a snack and she had put on a clean pinafore. She anticipated the visit with mixed

Just as it Was

feelings. Freda was the sister of her brother's first wife who had died two years ago after a long illness. Eva had been close to Sarah and she found Freda quite a different character to deal with. A knock at the door, Eva walked along the passage opened the door and there stood the couple. Suitcases in hand and carrying bags the two smiled and were invited to 'come in.' Eva was somewhat dismayed at the amount of luggage that they had brought, how long are they expecting to stay? she wondered.

'Take your coats off and hang them up, I'll see to the tea' she popped the kettle back onto the red embers of the fire to bring it back to the boil, no point using the gas ring when the fire was lit, in Eva's book that would be a mortal sin. 'You're not still boiling your kettle on the fire' Freda sniffed her disapproval as she settled down at the table. 'I've done with all that sooty kettles and pans, you don't put your pans on there as well do you?'

'Some of us have to look after our pennies,' Eva eyed the smart new dress and shoes that her sister in law was wearing before asking, 'do you take sugar or are you sweet enough?. Come on Harry, have a bite to eat we'll be having a proper meal when Phil gets in.' Harry picked up a sandwich and ate heartily, he ignored the remarks exchanged between the two women and concentrated on slurping his tea and stuffing himself with pastrys and cakes. Finishing their snack Eva cleared the table as Harry picked up one of the bags and took out a bulky parcel. 'There you are,' he said revealing a huge joint of pork and a large ham, 'that'll put some meat on your ribs.' Harry had often had something to say in the past on the

Just as it Was

'skinniness' of his sister and her family, his own ample proportions were much in contrast. In his youth as the oldest member of the family he had sparred in the bare knuckle rings for money to feed himself and his younger brothers and sisters who had been orphaned at an early age. In contrast to the careful and sometimes Spartan lifestyle of the rest of his family he now seemed to spend money pretty freely mixing with dubious characters and sometimes coming close to offending the arm of the law. In these times when rationing was still a fact of life Eva wondered where the meat had come from but she decided not to ask any questions it would help to feed them all and there was no point in causing trouble. The back door opened and as Julie came in she smiled as she saw her Uncle and going up to him she gave him a kiss. 'Now then tin ribs, you're growing up but you're not getting any fatter.'

I don't want to get fat Uncle Harry, I'm O.K. as I am.' She squiggled away from him.

'Are you getting enough to eat lass, are they feeding you at that hospital?'

'Course they are I'm not saying it's like Mum's cooking but it's O.K. stewed rabbit and Manchester tart, a bit like school dinners.' She went up to Freda and put her arms around her giving her a kiss. 'How are you Auntie, I like your dress.' She heard her mother give a 'hmnn' Mum had always denied herself the luxury of make up and fashionable clothes and even the presence of three daughters couldn't persuade her to take much of an interest in such things. Her hard childhood had instilled in her a desire for security and the only way to achieve that was to live as frugally as she could and to try and

Just as it Was

put something away for a rainy day. 'Are you coming to the races with us next week, do they give you any time off at that hospital where you work?'

'Yes of course I am Uncle, I've got Wednesday half day and all day Thurs off, and I've got my first month's pay.'

'We're alright then, you'll be able to treat us all.'

'It's only eight pounds Uncle Harry,' she laughed, 'I want to save up for a holiday as well, so if you've any tips for the St. Leger just let me know.' Race week was holiday week for a lot of the large concerns in Doncaster who closed down their premises. Some of the workers took the opportunity for a week at the sea-side. Great Yarmouth was a favourite destination for the railway workers as it was the furthest distance that they could travel on the privilege tickets which the company issued out to them and many chose to go there. Others preferred to stay at home and go to the races, Julie and her family caught the trackless into the town centre and after alighting from the bus they made their way to the Market Place. The pavements were crowded with women and girls dressed in summery cotton dresses and men who wore lightweight trousers and cotton shirts, ties and light jackets. All were in a merry mood as their town played host to an army of visitors, and the pubs and restaurants were doing a roaring trade. On the market top outside the Red Lion Hotel retired jockeys in brightly coloured silks were touting for custom as they gave tips for the princely sum of two shillings. Julie looked for the flamboyant figure of Prince Monolulu but he was probably somewhere nearer to the racecourse shouting the familiar 'Ah Gotta Hoss,' feathered headdress

Just as it Was

standing out like a beacon. Just at the far end of the fish market an escapologist, (there were rumours in the crowd that it was Houdini which was an impossibility because he had been dead for years.) was entertaining crowds of people as he valiantly and with great effort tried to release himself from the chains into which he'd been skillfully locked. There was a real carnival atmosphere and as they wandered around Eva said' let's go into the market hall and have a cup of tea before we make our way to the races.' It was dim in there and as her eyes adjusted to the light Julie recognized a familiar figure. Dressed in a bright green clinging style dress which emphasized her ample figure, and with a little red hat sporting a feather perched atop her blonde curls was Mrs Keogh, she from the hospital kitchen. The woman spotted Julie and waved, 'whose that?' Uncle Harry had seen the exchange and when Julie explained who she was he remarked, 'my she's a fine looking woman.' Freda wasn't having any of that 'come on Harry' she said taking his arm 'let's get this cup of tea.' The small cafe was crowded but they found a space where they all managed to squeeze in together. There was a buzz of conversation everyone was talking excitedly about their fancies on the turf. Race week was a welcome break for most who had been toiling in the pits, in the factories and working in the railway workshops. Doncaster was alive with energy; the atmosphere was friendly and full of expectation. 'Time that we were getting to the race course.' Phil gathered them all together and they made their way through the streets towards the town fields joining the large crowd which was on its way to the races. Excitement

Just as it Was

grew as they got nearer to the course. Automobiles with fashionably dressed passengers alighting from them pulled up outside the approach to the grandstand. Doncaster went upmarket when the elite of the racing world came to join them, the top jockeys, and trainers not to mention the wealthy owners dined and wined in the top hotels. The Danum, Mount Pleasant and numerous excellent inns such as The Red Lion in the market place. Owners of big houses rented them out to the rich and the famous and parties were lavishly laid on according to the size of the hosts win or of his bank balance. As she walked past Julie looked on enviously at the well dressed crowd who stood laughing and chatting together. Confidence oozed out from them their clothes, their expensive vehicles and fashionable hair do's and hats and sophisticated companions bore testimony to the fact that they were successful and wealthy. Just for a minute she wished that she had been born into those circumstances. She loved her family to bits but since going to grammar school and now going into nursing and mixing with other young women from all kinds of backgrounds she began to feel that there was more to life than back streets and cocoa and a visit to the picture house once a week. She dismissed the thoughts from her mind almost immediately as she thought about the advantages that she had over her older sisters she was a bit ashamed of herself and decided to enjoy what she had. It's no good wishing for things that I can't have it's race week, I'm going to make the most of it and enjoy myself. Drawing nearer to the course they saw sellers approaching racegoers to get them to buy Parkinson's butterscotch, Old Moores

Just as it Was

Almanacs, and race cards with tips marked off by the tipsters for their fancied winners. A little further along a couple of hopeful fresh faced eager young lads were trying to sell fruit, tomatoes and other items from the tailgate of an old lorry. 'Come on ladies get your bargains here, you're on to a sure winner with these. Get them before we sell out, only two bob for two pounds.' The crowds responded to them laughingly promising to buy some on the way out if they'd any money left. At last a sight of Prince Monolulu touting his tips as some people bantered with him and handed over their money trusting in his experience. The atmosphere was electric and Julie's spirits lifted as they all entered the Silver Ring. Her parents had been provided with 'Burgess Tickets' and Harry and Freda had generously offered to pay for their niece. There was a strict dress code and it was nice to mix with the eager crowd all looking forward to a pleasant and rewarding afternoon. The bookmakers were shouting the odds from their stands and the elated Harry and Phil had backed the first two winners, 'Come on let's have a glass of something in the marquee.' Phil led the way into the tent and as they made their way to the crowded bar they were once again challenged to find enough space to stay together. People were pushing and shoving a bit and as Harry turned quickly to rebuke someone who had nudged his elbow he tipped his glass sideways and some of the contents spilled onto the front of the green dress, which the lady behind him was wearing, immediately Julie recognized Mrs Keogh. Into the low cut dress flowed Harry's beer and as he flusteredly mopped away at it with his large handkerchief she blushed and the pair of

Just as it Was

them got more and more embarrassed. Harry was sweating and turning a vivid shade of red Mrs Keogh grew more and more uncomfortable she didn't know what to say. Freda was not at all pleased, Mrs Keogh was an attractive lady of ample proportions and her husband's close attentions to her irritated Freda. 'Give me that handkerchief Harry I'll deal with this.'

'Please I'm fine,'

'Mrs Keogh you'll smell like a brewery, here' said the other woman taking out a perfume spray which she generously proceeded to use on the poor hapless woman 'it's Helena Rubinstein.' Eva gave a snort of disapproval and almost fainted at the thought of the cost of such a thing she had a vague idea that it was something that only film stars and such used. 'That should do the trick' Freda put the spray back into her stylish handbag as Mrs Keogh looked anxiously around the tent. 'I've lost my husband in the crowd, he'd gone to buy some drinks.'

'I'll help you find him' Julie took her arm and together she and Mrs Keogh; red feather wafting from her hat and smelling like a mixture of a French Boudoir and a brewery, sailed off in search of Mr Keogh. Oh my goodness, Julie thought, she'll have a tale to tell in the kitchen tomorrow, I'll never live this down. After an eventful day they arrived home tired and dusty but happy. The women prepared tea, the tasty ham, which Harry had provided, was sliced up and with salad from Philips allotment and some of the tomatoes bought from the lads on the racecourse a meal was soon put on the table. The evening passed companionably the rest of the family who had

Just as it Was

spent the day together visiting friends had joined them. 'You missed a good day out you should have come with us.'

'If that's what you like dad but I've better things to do with my money.' Doris teased her father as they all sat together in the small sitting room. 'Aye I know lass, but it's only once a year and it's a good thing that it is.' Phil had come away losing after his early wins, 'perhaps I'll have better luck tomorrow. Them bookies have done alright today though, tic-tacking away, I don't know what they were saying to each other. They'd fistfuls o' money they've had a good day alright. It's all part of race week, sometimes you win and sometimes you lose' he looked down at the floor philosophically. 'Sometimes you're b----y second again' he was well known for just getting pipped at the post. They all laughed, tonight Mam had been to the off licence for her gill of beer and she brought a few bottles back for the others along with lemonade to make shandies for the girls. They had listened to each others stories and weary from the busy day at the races they were winding down in each other's company. Doris yawned 'come on we mustn't keep Mrs Thompson up, I'll be going to sleep here if I don't move.' The girls gathered up their overnight bags and made their way next door. Rosie was sitting in the gloomy gas lit living room curlers in her hair all ready to go up to bed, she smiled at the girls. Her home was behind the times in comparison with most of the others in the street. Utility furniture had given a new look to lots of homes during the nineteen forties but Rosie's solid oak table and sideboard bearing the black metal horses held by an almost naked young lad gave the home an old fashioned look. 'Had a good

Just as it Was

day?' she asked them. They all nodded wearily, 'it's a long time since I went to the races, I think I saw Edward there when I came to Doncaster on holiday as a little girl.' The girls looked at each other, would that be Edward the seventh, Queen Victoria's son! crikey that was a long time ago how old was Rosie? After chatting for a while they said goodnight to her, picked up the candlestick which she had already laid out; (for her home was still lit by gas light), they flickeringly made their way upstairs to the sparsely furnished bedroom where the iron bedsteaded beds were beautifully made up with crisp white linen. Snuggling down in no time at all the girls were fast asleep.

Just as it Was

6

Reaquaintance

Julie was standing at the huge sink in the sluice washing out many- tailed bandages. She was daydreaming as she stood there. She had been working on the surgical ward for almost five months and in January she would be going into the preliminary training school. Thoughts of living in the nurses' home were uppermost in her mind. Most of the staff lived in and there was a special friendliness between them which sometimes shut out the few who lived out. She looked forward in a way to becoming one of the inner circle though she knew that she would miss her family. Her sisters were both courting seriously and perhaps there would be a wedding before too long times were changing and the family as it now was would be so different. Anyway for the time being she might just enjoy leaving home and it was only for three months anyway. How would she get on in P.T.S. she had heeded the warnings that Sister Tutor was a dragon and it wouldn't be long before she found out. Her time on the ward had given her a real insight into what her chosen career was about, sometimes the days were uneventful, admissions, preparation, surgery, recovery, discharge. Coping with the dramas as she had done with Mrs Crowther's death and the train crash had been an ordination of fire for her. They were

Just as it Was

events that she would never forget but she had survived them and learnt to cope. It was rewarding most of the time to see people come in distressed and anxious and then to see them discharged in a better state of health and able to take up their lives again. She had only been allowed to perform very basic care but she had been allowed to observe and sometimes help with some of the procedures. When Staff Nurse Brown taught her to inject into an orange she felt that she was taking a real step forward. She knew that most of the intake in school would be completely oblivious to what happened on the wards and that perhaps she would be at an advantage. Julie was continuing this train of thought when Staff Brown came into the sluice, 'Nurse Spencer will you take Mrs Bamford a bedpan.' Julie sighed, she was always being taken from one job to another, she knew that if she went back into the long Nightingale ward that there would be someone else calling out to her to fetch this or take that away. Surely enough Sister Robson called to her 'Nurse Spencer, will you fetch a wheelchair and put Mrs Davidson into the bath please.' She had enjoyed a little respite when washing the bandages in the sluice and as she had gazed across the straight mile towards the nurses' home she had seen Dr John Gibson making his way over to the hospital. Their paths hadn't crossed since the encounter in casualty but now she was struck by him, his sturdy walk and his very handsome boyish almost manly figure had stirred up her interest in him. Julie wondered if their paths would ever cross again he had rescued her when she was upset that day and she would like to meet him again. Going back to the sluice she finished washing the bandages

Just as it Was

and hung them to dry on top of the sterilizer. Tonight after duty she was to take up Brenda Guy's invitation and join her and a few of the other nurses who were going to the dance at The Fairgrove, she had brought her toiletries, make up and one of her dresses along with a pair of strappy sandals with her that morning. Later she would go down to the cloakroom and get ready for her evening out. The remaining hours passed quickly and as half-past eight drew near the junior nurses gathered up the last of the cups and teaspoons from the lockers before going off duty. The teaspoons were set out to be counted by the nurse in charge and if one was missing no one was allowed to go off duty until it was found. 'Nurse Spencer, go and look on the lockers, one of the teaspoons is missing.' Sister Robson spoke sternly. This was one of the greatest misdemeanour's of all; that the day staff should mislay a teaspoon was considered a crime. Morning and evening the spoons were counted and if one was missing then the staff must remain until it was found. They all searched high and low, patients looked on disbelievingly as they watched. What a scandal, these girls have been on their feet all day, and they make a fuss about a missing teaspoon the patients muttered in disbelief. After running up and down the long wards all day caring and coping with all kinds of emergencies the disappearance of one teaspoon unbelievably blotted out everything else. The minutes passed by as they searched with no success then 'nurse, I've just found this in my bed' the very ancient Mrs Dodds held out the missing article, how it got there no-one knew but at last they could go off duty and as Julie hurried down to the cloakroom to change

Just as it Was

into her glad rags for the dance she heaved a sigh of relief. Released from the ward Julie tripped down the stone staircase, which led to the ground floor with impressive speed. She had arranged to meet some of the other nurses there and the search had made her late. Where've you been? Vera Sutton asked, she had now been moved to a medical ward but the friendship between the two had flourished. 'Missing teaspoon' Julie gasped as she quickly washed and applied her make up. The other girls watched the transformation as she pulled on the dress and quickly brushed her hair into a more glamorous style. They looked on appreciatively. Julie was tall and slim and with her chestnut coloured hair and green eyes, which positively danced with excitement when when the mood changed her. 'Come on I'm ready, we've only got a couple of hours I've to catch the last bus home.' Together they walked the short distance to 'The Fairgrove.' The night was cold and the odd lamp relieved the darkness of the empty streets. As they reached the hotel the lights shone out and the girls heard the sound of music from the three-piece band playing in an upper room. What would it be like? apart from the dances in the church hall which she had gone to with her sisters this was the first time that Julie had been to a real dance hall , if you could call it a dance hall. They walked into the small oblong shaped room, which was crowded with young and other not quite so young people. Some were on the dance floor doing a slow foxtrot as others stood looking on. Long windows looked over the shops and houses, which surrounded the hotel, and the odd flash of a car's headlight searched their way around the dimly lit room. 'Hang your coat up here' Vera

Just as it Was

and the others removed their jackets and scarves and hung them on the coat stands in the corner of the room. The hotel was close to the hospital and it was a popular night out for many of the nurses. As she looked around the room Julie recognised some familiar faces from the hospital. She looked again, was she mistaken or was that Colin the boy who she had danced with when out with her sisters at the church hall. He was dancing with a pretty dark haired girl chatting to her in a friendly and Julie thought somewhat intimate way. She was disappointed, after meeting him she had hoped that she would see him again because they had seemed to get on so well but after that first time he hadn't turned up at the local dance any more. The music stopped and after a while a Glenn Miller tune a quickstep, 'Chattanooga Chootoo' zipped through the room. 'Can I have this dance?' a red haired boy about the same height as Julie tapped her on the arm and as they moved onto the dance floor together Colin and his partner danced by and his and Julie's eyes met. To the strains of the lively music they passed by in a flash and Don who was partnering her took Julie sashaying across the dance floor. 'Wow that was good you're a great dancer,' at the end of the quickstep Don had walked Julie back to her friends, 'I haven't seen you here before.'

'No it's my first time, I like it, it's O.K.' The music struck up again this time a waltz, a favourite of Julies 'Down In The Glenn.' Suddenly before Don had a chance to ask her to dance with him again Colin stood before her and asked 'Can I have this dance?' She smiled and moved off with him, he held her firmly he was a few inches taller than Julie and she nestled

Just as it Was

nicely into his shoulder as the soft sound of the music flowed around the room. They danced in silence for a little while then Colin asked 'what are you doing all this way from home?'

'I'm working at the hospital, and this place is quite handy I've been there for five months.'

I'm up in Richmond I was called up to do my National Service, I'm on a thirty six hour pass.'

'You're a soldier, I can't believe it.'

'I'm eighteen now so I have to do it.'

'What about your job?'

'I'm a bricklayer, I hope that it'll be there when I get back.'

'I looked for you at the dance where you used to go I wondered where you'd got to'

He stretched out his arm gazing at her, 'I'm glad that we've met up again, I've thought about you a lot.'

Julie smiled, 'me too.' They moved together again dancing closely around the ballroom floor.

'We haven't seen much of you tonight.' Vera looked at her friend inquisitively, 'who's the lad?' It was half past ten and time that the girls were going for the last bus; they were taking their coats from the hangers. 'Just someone that I used to know he lives not far away from me so he's taking me home, we'll walk to the bus with you though, don't want you coming to any harm in the dark streets of Doncaster.' The three of them left and after catching the bus together Vera got off at her stop-calling goodnight to Colin and Julie. 'Which stop do you want?'

Just as it Was

'The next one' Julie said to the young man.

'I'll get off and walk you down the street, it's very dark and not safe for girls to be out on their own.'

'My Dad'll be waiting to meet me at the front door.'

'Lovely I'll be able to say hello to him.' As they got off the bus they crossed the main road which was almost empty of traffic. Here and there a lone cyclist pedalled his way home after working an afternoon shift for transport or for one of the local factories. The rear light of the bus disappeared into the black void. There was no moon tonight and as Colin tucked Julie's arm through his they hurried along the side road where she lived. 'When do you go back to camp?'

'Tomorrow afternoon, any chance of seeing you before I go?'

'I've got a half day morning, what about a walk in the dell?'

'I'll meet you there at half-past ten near the gates, O.K.?' they had neared the house.

'Julie is that you?' her father's voice rang out, he stepped out onto the pavement peering into the darkness. 'It's me Dad.'

'Is there somebody with you?'

'Dad this is Colin, he's brought me home from the dance, he only lives a few streets away.'

The young man stepped forward, he felt the scrutinizing gaze of Mr Spencer as he held out his hand. The older man took the hand, 'thanks lad,' he looks a decent sort he thought. 'Well it's getting late, I'd ask you in but it's our bed time so I'll say goodnight, perhaps we'll see you again.' Moving indoors he looked over his shoulder, 'don't be long Julie' he called. They

Just as it Was

stood alone on the pavement; Colin leaned forward and gave Julie a gentle kiss on the cheek. 'See you tomorrow' he said.

'I'll be there at ten-thirty don't be late.' She went indoors and locked the door behind her, she leant against it for a brief moment a satisfied look on her face. Walking into the living room she was greeted by her sisters who wanted to know all about the boy friend.

Promptly at half past ten Julie arrived at the gates of the Dell to find Colin already there. He smiled 'I didn't know whether you'd come or not.'

'Why did you think that?'

'I don't know, perhaps you've already got a boyfriend.'

'No I haven't.'

'A good looking girl like you, why not?'

'Never met anybody that I wanted to go out with more than once.'

'What about me?'

'You, oh! you're different, come on if we're going for a walk we better get on with it we haven't much time.' The Dell was dug out of an old quarry, in summer it was a blaze of colour and at weekends during the summer a brass band played in the bandstand around which Colin and Julie now walked. Streams which ran alongside the edges of the paths and little pools where goldfish sometimes swam and sometimes as today hid under the leaves of the decaying water lilies drew their attention. Surrounded by shrubs and lawns the couple

Just as it Was

had the place to themselves this morning and as they walked Colin took Julie's hand, 'I'm going to be away for quite a long time you know. I'll get some leave but it wont be very often.'

'How long will you be away?'

'It's two years altogether, but I've already done a few months.'

'Do you like it?'

'The lads are great, but the sergeant major's a bit of a bully, specially if anybody steps out of line, he had one lad whitewashing the stones that surrounded the parade ground, with a toothbrush because he hadn't got his kit in order. It's worse than working but it's got to be done.'

'I can't see girls standing for that, whitewashing with a toothbrush,' Julie laughed.

'I can't see you doing it, who'd want to make you anyway,' he looked at her tenderly. Laughing and pulling her along he said, 'come on I want to show you something.' They walked further into the Dell until they came to a pool with the figure of a young girl carved from stone; she was standing in the centre of the pool. 'I love that statue, I have since I was a small boy and me granddad used to bring me in here. I always thought she looked like the perfect girl, in fact I think that she looks like you.'

Julie was amazed. She laughed; 'like me you great goof, she looks cold to me and so am I, come on I'm freezing let's go and get a hot drink somewhere.' Colin took her hand, 'Julie I'm not kidding I'm really pleased that we've met up again.'

Just as it Was

'So am I.'

'If I write to you will you write back?'

'I think that's a good idea, yes I promise, I will write to you.'

'Come on then let's go and get that hot drink.' hand in hand they walked to the small grocer's shop where a couple of tables were set aside for passers-by who wanted to buy a hot drink and a home made scone. They gladly entered the cosy atmosphere and after ordering they chatted about their families and their work. 'I don't always want to be a brickie,' Colin told Julie, 'one day I'd like to go on my own. My uncle has a little jobbing business and he's doing pretty well I'd like to do something like that.'

'You're ambitious, nothing wrong with that I feel the same way,' Julie picked up her cup and sipped the comforting hot liquid. Too soon they had to say goodbye promising that he would write Colin left Julie as she reached her home. Both had things to do she was going on duty at the hospital and he was going back to camp in North Yorkshire. 'I'll be home at Christmas' he told her.

Just as it Was

7

Frugal Celebration

Chris Walker looked up from the book that she was reading as Julie and Vera Sutton walked into the sitting room of the nurses' home. 'I thought that you two were going into town to do some Christmas shopping in your off duty.'

'There's not much point, we're waiting for pay day and window shopping doesn't appeal to me.' Vera sank into one of the comfortable armchairs and Julie sat opposite to her. Since the two had been moved onto different wards they had seen little of each other and they were having a catch up. 'Soon be Christmas Eve, I love Christmas Eve I hope I'm not working.'

Julie looked at Vera before saying 'Christmas day's best for me, opening presents and all the family together I love it.'

'It's alright when you're a kid, but me and Dennis like to go out dancing, Christmas Eve's more fun.'

'Are you and Dennis going to get engaged then? Chris had listened to lurid tales from Vera about their romantic goings on in the back of his car. Steamy sessions in the little Austin Seven which sometimes broke down in the most isolated of places. Vera had been obliged to walk several miles to get help on some occasions. The stories were often amusing but when Vera went into detail they were not suitable for the ears

Just as it Was

of Julie who was still an innocent young girl. She changed the subject 'Christmas in hospital's not bad for the staff and we do our best for the patients, that's those who can't go home. The police choir come in to sing carols on Christmas Eve and we trim the wards up a bit. The Mayor does a round of all the patients with matron and their little entourage and Santa hands out presents. to them all.' Julie was listening eagerly she knew that she would miss being amongst her family on Christmas day but perhaps it wouldn't be so bad quite an experience in fact. Chris went on 'the surgeons come in at lunchtime to carve the turkeys they're always a bit of fun; that's the surgeons not the turkeys. Of course they go home then to their own Christmas dinner but if possible later on all the doctors and nurses on the ward have a little party with everyone bringing something towards it. It can be quite a nice time. 'Julie thought that Christmas working in hospital might be something to look forward to and not only that after Christmas she would be going into P.T.S. and her three year training would begin in earnest. There was also the fact that Colin would be coming home and after exchanging letters the two were very much looking forward to seeing each other again.

It was the week before Christmas and the off duty had been put up; everyone was on duty on Christmas day Julie had the evening off on Christmas Eve. 'You'll be going and coming on the bike there'll be no buses running' her mother was ironing in the small living room as Julie was getting ready to go back on duty. 'What are you going to do on Christmas Eve?'

Just as it Was

'Colin's coming home Mum, I wondered if I could bring him to meet you and Dad?'

'I've a lot to do yet to get ready for Christmas day, the tree's not up yet.'

'We can do that, he'll just take us as he finds us.'

'Oh alright then, if your Dad agrees.' The two youngsters had been exchanging letters and Colin was now considered to be well in. With a family of six Mrs Spencer had her hands full. She was a stickler for routine and her house-cleaning programme was carried out religiously every week. With the added work of making Christmas puddings, pastries and cakes, and planning the Christmas day lunch which this year was to be a nice big chicken she was feeling hard pressed. Babs and Doris did what they could to help but their work in the factories; Doris at Peglers where they had made munitions during the war and Babs at Briggs Motor Bodies, they hadn't much spare time. On her day off Julie had helped where she could this week she had to clean the bedrooms. There was Sherry the dog to walk and Dad and John to feed when they came in from work, so all in all it was a busy household. There was little time for the finer things in life. As in many families the war years had brought more financial security. Women were working in the factories fully employed in making ammunition for the troops to use on the battle front. The early years after the war saw people's expectations increase. They had made do and mended for six years and they were now going to seize the chance of a better life. However it didn't happen in the Spencer household. Eva had the memories of her childhood behind her; she opened a post office account

Just as it Was

and put something away each week so that she would always have something to fall back on. As a result the furniture had seen better days and the ill matched crockery would do as far as she was concerned. There was a china tea set in the kitchen cupboard but it was reserved for very special occasions, something similar to a visit from royalty perhaps!

Julie hurried up through the hospital corridors to the top of the drive on Christmas Eve. There he was waiting for her and as he shyly took her hand she felt a little bit awkward it was weeks since she had seen him. 'Do I get a kiss?' She held up her cheek to him as he brushed her face with his lips. 'I've been dying to see you, I've been thinking about you all the time that I've been away, and I've got something to tell you.'

'What is it?'

'Not here I'll tell you later.'

Julie looked up towards the road, she pulled his arm, 'come on run the bus is here, we don't want to miss it.' They took the trolley bus to Wysten there was no chance to talk, Colin stood holding on to the upright pole near Julie's seat as the woman sitting next to her talked at length about her daughter who was a nurse in Leeds. The two youngsters kept glancing at each other, the woman smiled at Colin and continued to talk to Julie. Finally they arrived at their stop and as they got off the bus the cold air whipped around them causing Julie to shiver Colin pulled her towards himself and they walked quickly, arms linked. 'Ooh I'm so cold, come on, let's run' they ran down the street hand in hand towards the Spencer's

Just as it Was

home. Their knock on the door was soon answered and after taking off their outdoor things in the draughty dark passage the warmth from the coal fire greeted them as they walked into the living room. The family were washing up after their evening meal as the two arrived Babs had cleared the table and Mum and Doris were in the kitchen at the old stone sink. Mrs Spencer came through, 'hello' she said taking the kettle off the fire, John's in the bath upstairs and he's run all the hot water off so I'll have to boil the kettle for some water to finish the washing up.'

'Mum this is Colin.'

'Well I've heard a lot about you from our Julie, come in and sit down, we'll soon get things done then we'll be able to come and sit down with you.' Mr Spencer got up from his wooden armchair and held out his hand to Colin. 'It's nice to meet you again lad.' he shook the hand of the young man who smiled and then sat nervously in the proffered chair. 'Would you like a cup of tea?' Mrs Spencer hands on hips, tea towel hanging from one of them came back from the kitchen where she had hotted up her washing up water. She stood in the doorway, which led off the living room. 'No thank you,' Colin replied politely. Doris had come through from the kitchen recognising the young man from the dances, which they had all gone to in the Church Hall, she approached Colin. 'It's nice to see you again, Julie told us that you were in the army, we missed you at the dances.' The conversation was interrupted as John came downstairs. Colin stood up as Julie introduced the two. they shook hands and John asked 'what's it like in the army?' it would be his turn to go in a couple of years time. Now

Just as it Was

sixteen years old John was working in the railway workshops where his father worked and with three girls in the family he thought that a bit more male company would be a nice change. All that the girls talked about were boyfriends and dancing and the latest films although since Julie had begun her nursing career he didn't see so much of her. He was the apple of his mother's eye, but again that sometimes caused him problems so a spell up in North Yorkshire with a bunch of lads might be just the life for him. 'I can't wait to get out, I want to get on with my life I'd like to get back to my job and back to Doncaster' Colin sneaked a look at Julie who was picking up some Christmas cards which had arrived that day as he said this. Babs had gone upstairs and now she came back into the room dressed, to go out, make up on and ready to face the cold night air. Her boyfriend lived in a small village on the outskirts of Doncaster, she had promised to go over to see him and his parents this evening as tomorrow he would be spending part of Christmas day with the Spencers. 'Sorry to be going out but it's been nice to meet you,' she said to Colin 'I wont be long anyway I might see you when I get back I'm really just going to deliver some presents to Derek's family.' Mr Spencer who had immersed his attention to the sports section of the evening paper looked up and thought to himself what nice manners the lad had as he stood up and said cheerio to Babs. He shook his paper and settled down to read it again but as Babs called out 'cheerio' and opened the door to go out into the street a blast of cold air blew in through the sitting room door. 'Shut that, Bl---y door' Mr Spencer grumbled 'it's like a railway station in here.' Julie

Just as it Was

knew better than to comment she knew her Dad well but as she looked across at Colin she could see that he was uncomfortable. 'Don't worry, he doesn't bite' she whispered, the two were now sharing the little settee, which was just about big enough for them if they sat closely together. The other women were making preparations towards Christmas dinner in the kitchen and John had gone back upstairs. 'It's O.K. my Dad swears sometimes.'

'I think he forgot you were here.' Colin looked anxious.

'It's not that, I've got to talk to you Julie, I want to know something.'

'We can't talk, Mum'll be in from the kitchen any minute, I promised to decorate the tree I better go and get the rest of the stuff from upstairs we'll talk later.' She soon returned with the box of baubles and John came with her carrying down the small ancient Christmas tree. The colourful paper chains had already been put up in the small living room where the family ate, relaxed and lived out their lives. Christmas cards from relatives and close friends were standing on the sideboard everything happened in this room while the tiny front parlour stood icily dusted and polished, waiting to be used on special occasions. 'Here we are' the tree was an almost revered, much-treasured object in the Spencer family. It was just over two foot high and its branches, which looked as though they might originally have been flu brushes, were now almost bare. This was in part due to the fact that the candles, which were held by candle-holders which clipped onto them, when lit went up in flames at least once every Christmastime. No serious damage was ever done but each year the tree was a little

Just as it Was

worse for wear. Although all declared that the tree ought to be replaced it had never happened. Mrs Spencer was in charge of the purse and she did not throw her money about. The tree was good for a few years yet they were told. 'Come on Colin, it's our job to do this, let's make this tree look a bit festive.' The young man eyed the task with some doubt 'I think you better do it,' he said shyly to Julie. He was feeling overawed by meeting so many of Julie's family and was happy just to sit there and watch. As she bent over the tree hanging the baubles on the branches Julie exclaimed and gave him the history of some of the items as she hung them. Year after year they had come out of the box, the little silver and bronze bird with coloured feathers spreading from his tail and the bright red Santa that one of them had fashioned out of a clothes peg when small. Every item was familiar and held memories of past Christmases. Colin watched her tenderly, as excitement gave her a special look. Her expression was innocent and beautiful and he was moved that this very lovely girl was interested in him. He wanted to hold her, to take her in his arms and tell her how he had thought of her constantly when he was in the army barracks. Hopefully they would get some time on their own tonight and he would be able to tell her these things he wanted to tell her of his plans. 'Ready for the tinsel now,' even that was looking a bit threadbare as it was wound round and around giving shape to the tree. At last it was done, 'better not light the candles this year, there wont be any tree left.' Julie stood back looking at her handiwork, 'what do you think of it Colin?'

Just as it Was

'It's the most beautiful thing I've ever seen.' he said. Julie laughed, 'you don't have to say that you know.' Doris and her mother came in from the kitchen 'That looks alright, we've almost done, we're getting on better than I thought we would.' they came into the living room and sat down. The evening was wearing on and still Colin and Julie hadn't had a chance to talk, she wondered what he had to tell her but she realised that she wasn't going to find out yet. Mr Spencer was at last giving some attention to the others in the room while the youngsters had been decorating the tree he had alternately been snoozing and reading his paper. He now stood up, stretched and spoke to them all, 'how about I nip round to the off licence for some beer and we'll all have a drink together,' He often went up to the Swan at the top of the street for a pint with his friends but tonight he thought that it would be good to stay in and have a bit of a party with the family when in the mood he was very sociable. The presents were wrapped, the tree and the decorations were up and the meal was prepared as far as was possible. The bird was on the stone slab in the cellar keeping nice and fresh and the house had been cleaned from top to bottom. It was agreed by all that his was a good idea so slipping on his jacket he went towards the back door 'fetch a shovel of coal up from the cellar John, lets have a nice fire, it's a cold night,' he called as he went outside on his way to the off licence. He brought back some bottles of best bitter, a jug of ale for Mum and the girls to make shandies and a few packets of potato crisps. Eddie Spencer liked a little flutter on the horses now and then and this week he had won a few bob and he

Just as it Was

intended to spend it on giving his family a good Christmas Eve. 'What are your family doing tonight?' Julie was clearing away the boxes which had held the Christmas tree decorations. 'Pretty much the same, getting ready for tomorrow, there's going to be seven of us, grandma and granddad are staying, they've been coming for a few years now.'

'Think about me then when you're all enjoying yourselves. It's the first Christmas day that I've spent away from my family I'll be thinking about you all tomorrow.'

'Here we are,' as Dad arrived at the back door, there was a knock at the front of the house. Babs had arrived home, she was excited and more than a little flushed. After hanging up her coat in the passageway she came through to the living room where they were all gathered. She held out her left hand three small diamonds sparkled under the electric light and she described to them how Derek had romantically proposed to her, choosing Christmas Eve to make it even more special. 'Mam get that sherry bottle out, we need something a bit stronger than beer to celebrate with.' The family surrounded Babs hugging and kissing and congratulating her as Colin looked on. Mr Spencer raised his glass, 'Congratulations to Babs and Derek, and a very happy Christmas to everybody. Lets put some music on and have a bit of a dance.' The gramophone was wound up, the table and chairs were pushed up against the back wall and as the sound of lively music rang through the home Mr Spencer lead the jollifications with his wife tut-tutting and complaining about the state of the living room until after a couple of sherries she sat down on the old

Just as it Was

horse hair settee and fell fast asleep despite the noise. After a hesitant few minutes Colin joined in the dancing. At first he just tapped his foot gently to the music but as the rest of the family let all their inhibitions go he stamped and twirled and swung his legs like the rest of them to the strains of 'When Father Papered The Parlour.' and many other lively tunes. Mum woke up eventually and shook her head at the sight of the living room. She took in the scene which by this time had begun to quieten. They had all enjoyed the music and the dancing and were laughing at antics they had performed. 'Fancy me falling asleep what time is it? quarter to eleven, Julie it's time you were in bed you've got to work tomorrow, it's time that we were all thinking about bed come on let's put this room straight.' Doris and Babs took the glasses and plates into the kitchen as Julie fetched Colin's coat. After saying his goodbyes to the rest of the family and promising to come again after Mr Spencers effusive invitation the two walked towards the passageway, they closed the living room door behind them. The passage was in darkness. 'I hope you've enjoyed yourself,' Julie took the young man's hands in hers.'I always enjoy myself when I'm with you.' She looked up at him smiling and he took his hands out of hers and put his arms around her, he looked at her, then pulled her more closely to himself. Looking down he bent his head towards hers and very gently touched her lips with his. A surge of passion passed between them and they were clinging together as Colin kissed her again this time with urgency. Neither of them wanted to part but they pulled away from each other

Just as it Was

swiftly as the door opened and Mr Spencer called. 'Come on now Julie, don't take all night it's bedtime.'

'Wont be long Dad' she looked at Colin quizzically, 'what is it you wanted to talk about'

'It's too late now we'll talk about it next time.'

'Come on, I want to know what it is.'

He looked at her directly, 'I want to emigrate, I want to go to Canada when I come out of the army I want to live abroad and I want you to come with me.'

Just as it Was

8

Early Beginnings

The Badminton Hall in the nurses home was buzzing with the sound of young women's voices. About twenty of them were awaiting the arrival of Sister Tutor who was to welcome them into the preliminary training school. Julie found an empty chair next to a rosy-cheeked small blonde girl who looked in a bit of a dither. 'Is it O.K. if I sit here?' The girl was obviously feeling abandoned and she looked relieved as she spoke, 'I wish you would, I don't know anyone here I'm not very sure about all this.'

'You'll be fine, I'm Julie by the way, Julie Spencer, don't worry, there's nothing to be afraid of. I've been working on the wards since last July till I was old enough to start training, we're all in the same boat today.'

'My name's Margaret Williams, and I think my boat's rocking a bit,' she laughed at her attempt to make a joke of it. 'I'm worried, I don't think that I'm going to like it.'

'Give it a chance Margaret, you'll soon get to know everybody I know how you feel, I know what I felt like the first time that I was faced with everybody in the dining room.' Julie looked around the room where different individuals were standing or

Just as it Was

sitting on their own as the more gregarious ones got together. 'Where do you live?'

'With me Mum and Dad and little brother out at Woodlands, I'm not sure how I'll feel living away from home.'

'I'm a bit the same, I've been able to live out up to now but in a way I feel that it might be fun living in. A lot of the staff who live in seem to enjoy it when they're talking about what goes on in the nurses' home, to tell you the truth I feel that I'm missing something. Perhaps we'll like living in.' There was a stir as a woman in a blue dress, white apron and on her head an immaculate flowing folded linen square which came to a point at the back came into the hall The girls stood and she acknowledged them and then quickly asked them to sit down before she introduced herself. 'My name is Sister Freeman welcome to this hospital, I will be taking you for lectures along with the senior tutor Sister Deane whom you will meet later. We want all of you nurses, (Margaret leaned over to Julie and whispered in her ear 'blimey that was quick we haven't even got our caps and aprons yet.') to feel that you can come to either of us with any problems that you have. Many of you will be living away from home for the first time and you might find it difficult to adjust. We are not ogres and you can approach us with anything that concerns you. Now is there anything that you would like to ask.'

'Please Sister will we be able to go out in the evenings?' the question was from a dark haired slim girl who had a north-east accent.

Just as it Was

'Of course you will, this isn't a prison you know. However you must be in by ten-thirty. The doors will be locked after that time.' She smiled 'now if there are no more questions we will show you to your rooms. As you leave the hall today the home sister and her helpers will take you up to the floor where the rooms are. Most of them are doubles so if you could each choose a partner before we set out it might be the best way forward.'

'Will you share with me please?' Margaret looked pleadingly towards Julie.

'Why not,' the girl looked normal enough, pleasant enough, and the two of them had seemed to bond quite quickly. 'Later' went on the tutor 'you will go over to the sewing room to be fitted out with your uniform, we will show you around the grounds and parts of the hospital and at three o'clock we will come back here and meet Sister Deane. Oh yes you will of course be given lunch in the nurses dining room where a table is set-aside for the P.T.S for the length of your stay in the school. Now then nurses, follow me' Sister Freeman climbed the stairs in the nurses home up to floor three, this is the area where your rooms are and this large room at the end is where Matron is housed. The area referred to was large with a balcony, which overlooked the hospital tennis court. 'Crikey' said a big girl with a South Yorkshire accent to the others, 'They're putting us out of the way up here aren't they.I thought I was getting a bit a freedom leavin' home but it looks as though we're right under Matron's eye.'

'You never know your luck, she might invite you in for tea if you're a good girl' said one of the others.

Just as it Was

'Now girls, remember that from today you are part of this hospital and you will be judged on that. Please let us have no more of this banter, Miss Ferguson will not appreciate it I will leave you to get your rooms in order and your belongings put away.'

There was a small wardrobe, two single beds, neatly made up with smooth pale green bedspreads lying neatly over the sheets and pillowcases and a chest of drawers. A washbasin, with a mirror hanging on the wall was a nice addition Julie thought as she looked into the mirror and preened. A small table and two chairs were provided presumably thought Julie for us to do our written work. 'Not very big, is it?' Margaret sat on one of the beds. 'I expect they're all the same, I don't think we've got a choice, we're only here for a few months anyway and we wont be spending much time in this room. Come on Margaret lets unpack.'

'What's it like on the wards?' Margaret was slowly putting her things into drawers, she was still feeling uneasy as she asked Julie the question.

'It depends, it's different everyday, sometimes it's pretty quiet others it's hectic. There's always someone to ask if you want to know anything, don't worry you'll go on the wards to do some practical work while you're in school, then you'll find out for yourself. I'm sure you'll be O.K.' Finishing the task of putting their few belongings away, which didn't take long the two girls, made their way to the small kitchen, which was further along the corridor. They found a few of the other new recruits gathered. Julie scrutinised the group they were a disparate lot. Some of them had experience in hospital

Just as it Was

previously as nursing orderlies and they now wanted to train. Others had come from office work and one or two like she, had come straight from school having reached the required age. There were all kinds of accents, West Yorkshire, Geordie, a couple of Irish girls and several from South Yorkshire. The conversation was pleasant as cups of tea were handed around. We'll soon get to know one another it's going to be interesting I'm looking forward to it she thought. After lunch and a visit to the sewing room for their uniform the girls went back to the Badminton Hall, which was to be their lecture room and where they were now to meet Miss Deane. 'I know someone who trained here' Jean, the girl from West Yorkshire said. 'I was told to look out for the senior tutor; she doesn't think much of some of the student nurses. 'The girl put on a loud voice, 'not like we were in our day Miss Freeman, we were ladylike, I'm afraid they fall short, either pregnant or prostitutes.' The other girls gasped, Miss Deane had just come into the room and had heard every word; walking up to the girl she faced her. 'Prove me wrong' she said, 'and now all of you sit down.' The next few weeks were a whirl of lectures and written and practical experience. The student nurses were introduced to Chubby' the skeleton who was of an indeterminate sex. They were surprised and overawed at the intricacies of the human frame and even more so when the muscles and the organs were introduced. 'I thought the Islets of Langerhans' were in Barbados Margaret laughed. (The Islets of Langerhans are situated in the pancreas and produce insulin.) The work was concentrated and regular tests were set. Some of the students had second thoughts about a

Just as it Was

nursing career and the numbers dwindled. There were moonlight flits, and some of them just didn't come back after a day off. At the end of the three months at least half of them had disappeared. 'Are you going to the dance at the aerodrome tomorrow night' a few of the students were sitting in Audrey's room one evening as they discussed their day over a cup of coffee and a packet of custard creams. Invitations were sent out to the nurses from time to time and home sister had extended this one to the P.T.S. 'I don't think my Mum'll let me,' Janet a seventeen year old from Barnsley said.

'She'll never know, you don't have to ask her.'

'Do you want to go?'

'What'll it be like?'

'Don't know shall we go and find out?' Several of the girls decided to go and a small vehicle was to come from the camp and pick them up. By special arrangement a late pass had been given to them and they were allowed to stay out until eleven o'clock. The girls spent time discussing what they would wear. They looked into their wardrobes and lent and borrowed and helped each other with hair do's what would it be like. The aerodrome at Finningley had played a major part as had all the airfields in Britain in the second world war. Very few civilians had access to these places. They were still manned and operational and the girls felt that there was a mystique about them and didn't know what to expect. Eagerly on the night they took great care about their appearance and about half a dozen of them arrived at the appointed place to

Just as it Was

be taken to the airfield. Julie and Margaret had gone along and as they walked into the building where the dance was to be held they were struck by the lack of glamour. A miserable greyness hung over the place and they felt lost in the vastness of it. God how had those young men felt when they were stationed here miles away from home, and going on bombing raids night after night. There was no official reception but the driver showed them where to hang their coats and they wandered into the room, which had been set aside for the dance. A couple of dozen airmen and females were dancing to a trio of drums cello and keyboard. 'It's not what I expected 'Margaret said. 'Me neither said Julie.'

'Can I have this dance?' a young man in uniform approached her, as they danced he told her that he was a regular and had been there during the war. Julie got the impression that he would have been glad to get away from there and when he asked and she told him that she had a boyfriend he thanked her for the dance and she returned to Margaret who had been dancing with another airman. 'I get the feeling that these lads would rather be at home with their girl friends.'

'It's gloomy in here' Julie said.'bit miserable really, I always thought that aerodromes were exciting places, ah well, soon be time for home.' After that the girls were careful about the invitations that they accepted and in truth there was very little time for getting out and about. The nicest part of being in P.T.S was the get togethers and the chat that they had in each other's room and in the nurses' sitting room. One day they were talking when Audrey came in. 'You're looking a bit

Just as it Was

down today' one of the other girls said to her, 'what's the matter?'

'I'm alright, just a bit fed up.'

'Is it your love life?'

Audrey laughed 'what love life, I haven't seen Jim all week, haven't heard from him either, I went to tea last week and I haven't seen him since.' Audrey was a quiet pretty girl, she came from a working class family who lived in one of the less well-recognised parts of Doncaster. She had met her boyfriend at one of the local dance halls and they had dated for a few months. The others had followed the story of their courting interestedly as girls do and the conclusion was that the pair seemed to be very much in love. 'I think that I know what the trouble might be with Jim,' Iris lived locally not very far from where Jim's family were. It was a nice residential area, the husbands who lived there worked in banks and offices and some of them ran their own businesses. 'Jim's mother is a very toffee nosed snob. Audrey's background wont be good enough for her son, she doesn't come from the right part of town.'

'Who does she think she is, Lady Docker?'

'Can't be doing with people like that, you're better off without him if he listens to his mother you've got a career in front of you anyway Audrey. Forget about him if that's it.'

Sister Deane was speaking to the students in the clinic where they had performed their practical work and learnt the procedures. 'Well girls I'm delighted to tell you that you have

Just as it Was

been one of the best groups that we have had here for a long time. Your exam results are excellent and I hope that you will keep the standard up when you go onto the wards. Don't forget what you have been taught and always treat the patients and their relatives as you would treat your own families. Don't forget, there are young doctors out there who will flatter you and pursue you but always get their instructions about the patient's treatment in writing. If push comes to shove and things go wrong you will be on your own, you wont have a leg to stand on. Now off you go and good luck with your careers, your placements are posted in the Badminton hall.'

'Can't wait, she's not such a bad old stick after all, is she?' Margaret said.

Just as it Was

9

Colin On leave

Margaret and Julie were working on the same floor, Julie was on men's surgical and her friend was on the female ward. They had become good friends and each had done well in the exams. 'Guess what I did today,' the two were on their way to lunch. 'I helped staff to do a bowel washout on Mrs Birtwhistle she's going to theatre on Thursday it was really interesting.'

'Do you mind,' Julie laughed at her friend 'I'm going for my lunch, there are some subjects that are best left alone just before a meal.' It was true that the less presentable face of nursing took a bit of stomaching, she was able to switch off completely when necessary. Unfortunately Margaret was one of those who couldn't and she was often accused of putting people off their food as she talked about unsuitable topics.

As Julie arrived home that evening her mother said 'there's a letter for you.' Julie had arrived home to find the family having their night-time drink. Bedtime was early in the Spencer household especially during the week when they were all working. Half past nine was getting on a bit and ten o'clock was definitely late. Taking off her coat Julie picked up the letter from the sideboard and looked at the postmark, it was

Just as it Was

from Richmond where Colin was stationed. She opened the letter and read it, 'he's coming home next weekend.'

'That's nice, have you got some off duty?'

'I'll have to ask but I'm not sure that I'll be able to get the weekend off.' Julie and Colin had written to each other regularly and after realising at Christmas how each of them felt about the other they had started courting seriously. The time that they had spent together was very little and Julie hoped that she would be able to get off duty while he was home. 'I've got something to tell you, and to ask you,' Babs who was helping to clear away the supper pots smiled at her sister. 'Me and Derek are getting married in September and we'd like you to be a bridesmaid.'

'Oh sis' that's wonderful, course I'd love to be a bridesmaid. I've never been one before. What shall I wear and who else is going to be one?'

'Come on girls, time to talk about that tomorrow' said their mother looking at the clock.

'Sister would it be possible for me to have my off duty at the weekend next week?' Julie was reporting for duty and took the opportunity as soon as she could to ask for the time off. It would be a chance for her and Colin to talk about things, they saw so little of each other that there wasn't a lot of chance for their relationship, or whatever it was to develop. When he was on leave she wasn't always able to see much of him. 'I don't think that it will Nurse Spencer, Nurse Booth has already asked for it, she has made a booking so I'm afraid that it's

Just as it Was

impossible.' The girl looked dejected. 'What I could do is give you a two to four on Saturday and half day afternoon on Sunday, would that help.'

'Oh thank you, I think that it will' Julie said. She went off into the ward, it was busy at the moment and the night staff had admitted three patients during the night. The last one had been sent up from accident and emergency only an hour ago. He was a young man twenty years old and his name was Norman. He had severe abdominal pain and after examining him up on the ward the R.S.O. (Resident Surgical officer.) suspected a perforated appendix and wanted him in theatre straight-away. Norman was clammy and his tongue and lips were as dry as paper. His colour was poor and staff nurse was extremely concerned at his condition. Apparently he lived with his mother, just the two of them together in the house and he had been unable to rouse her to get help during the night. 'This is going to be touch and go, I think I'm going to find pus in there when I open him up' the Dr said. Norman was wheeled down to theatre on a trolley and Julie was told to go down with him. She took his hand and he opened his eyes and looked at her hazily. 'I'm going to die aren't I nurse?'

'Don't you dare' then she smiled 'we wont let you' she said. After leaving Norman in the care of the anaesthetist and the theatre staff Julie returned to the ward and with help from one of the other nurses she made up the op. bed (the patients own ward bed made up in a special way to ease the transfer from trolley to bed after surgery.) ready for the young man's return. After a couple of hours the office phone rang, 'Mr Shaw is ready to come back to the ward, could you send a

Just as it Was

nurse down please' the theatre sister said. Once again Julie made her way this time into the recovery room. Norman was still heavily under the anaesthetic and totally unaware, he had an intravenous saline drip running into his arm, she and the porter got him back onto the ward and with help they lifted him onto the bed. Shortly afterwards the surgeon came onto the ward. He was concerned about the young man and told Sister Lester that he had found pus in the cavity and that the lad would be worse before he was better. The intravenous fluids were continued and heavy doses of penicillin were given. Julie went off duty that evening hoping against hope that he would still be there when she went back next day. For the next couple of days he drifted in and out of consciousness, he had been vomiting nasty brown fluid and a paralytic ileus was diagnosed. (A rare complication particulary when prolonged handling of the gut is involved.) Nothing by mouth but strict mouth toilet was essential and as his temperature soared tepid sponges were given regularly. They were anxious days and as his Mum sat by his bedside prayers were muttered and everyone nervously hoped that he would recover. The week passed and as Julie went off on her half day Sunday there were slight signs of improvement. The whole ward, staff and patients had been willing Norman to recover and surely he was on the right road now.

'Did you enjoy yourself last night?' Colin hadn't arrived home until early evening and by that time Julie was back on duty. He had gone for a drink with one of his old school friends and now he had come to meet his girl friend at her parents' home.

Just as it Was

'I'd rather have been with you, we're not going to have much time together, what do you want to do?'

'What can you do in Doncaster on a Sunday afternoon?'

'We could go for a walk.'

'I'm tired, we've been very busy on the ward.'

'How about going to visit someone?'

'Who do you want to go and visit?, I'll tell you what, let's catch a bus out to Bawtry, we can take a picnic and walk by the river.'

'That's a fantastic idea' Colin picked Julie up and gave her a kiss before she went through into the kitchen to begin packing sandwiches and cakes together. The other younger members of the family were out and Julie's parents were snoozing as the radio played to itself. Mum was resting after the chores and Dad was rendered into sleep by the couple of pints that he had drunk at the Swan before Sunday Dinner. 'Nearly ready now' she called 'just got to comb my hair and get my jacket and we're off.' There was a typical sultry Sunday afternoon air about the day as the almost empty trolley bus took them into town. The walk to catch the connection to the little market town was made through deserted streets flanked by shop windows sporting their goods to non-existent buyers. Julie would have liked to browse. 'No time to stop and look, we might miss our connection, come on we're going for a picnic.' Arriving in the little market town they threaded their way through the streets making their way to the riverbank. 'This is better' the land opened up around them and occasionally a playful breeze caught the bushes causing them

Just as it Was

to dance and rustle happily. Stepping through the grass along the river bank Julie let out a yell as a skylark flew up startling her. Colin gave a chortle and held her steadily, 'not frightened of a little bird, are you?' with manly concern he took her hand.

'I've got a phobia about flying feathers.'

'What else don't I know about you?'

'Only a thousand and one things, I'm a bit complicated.'

'I'm looking forward to getting to know everything,' Julie recovered and they walked on and came to a smooth grassy area where they flopped down readily with the picnic bags. There were only a few people about although the day was warm and sunny. Further down the banking a few youths, jumped in and out of the water, yelling at each other and having fun. They were far enough away not to bother the young couple and Colin rolled up his jacket and invited Julie to lay her head on it as he sat down beside her. He gazed at her 'you know that you have the loveliest eyes I've ever seen.'

Julie laughed up at him. 'Where did you get that line from?'

'Just because I'm a Yorkshire man it doesn't mean that I have no romance in my soul.' He picked up a piece of grass and tickled her under the chin. She rolled over onto her stomach. 'Grab that buttercup and see if I like butter' she said. He threw himself down on the grass beside her holding the yellow flower under her chin then drew her closer; tossing the buttercup away he threw his arm across her back and was pulling her to face him when suddenly there was a large clap of thunder. Absorbed in each other they hadn't noticed the darkening skies, the clouds opened and they were soaked

Just as it Was

through in no time. 'Quick head under that little bridge' Colin grabbed Julie by the arm, picking up their belongings the two ran for cover as quickly as they could. 'Phew that's put a damper on things, just look at you you're wet through.' It was true she was soaked to the skin her dress clung to her body, and her wet hair formed a dark frame around her face highlighting her youthful complexion and her firm sculptured jawline. Looking at her Colin took her face between his hands, 'you should always have wet hair, you look absolutely stunning.' This was flattering but what was happening she looked down and Colin put his finger under her chin and lifted her lips to his as an irresistible force drew them together. They kissed passionately as he ran his hands over her soddened clothes and felt the firmness of her thighs and the soft lift of her breasts. She resisted, drawing away, 'please Colin that's enough.'

'I love you, I can't help myself.'

'Colin we're young, not only that, you're miles away in North Yorkshire and I've just started my nursing career.'

'What are you saying, don't you want us to be together.'

'I'm just saying let's take our time, don't rush things.'

'I'll be going back tomorrow morning and I don't know how long it'll be before I'm home again.'

'If you really love me you can wait. We mustn't spoil; things Colin.'

'That's the last thing that I want, I really love you Julie.'

Just as it Was

'And I think that I love you Colin, but you're going too fast for me, look it's stopped raining, the sun's out again, let's see if there's anything left in these bags worth eating.'

The first thing that Julie did after reporting for duty on Monday morning was to look in the ward at the place where Norman's bed was. Could that really be him! sitting up in bed wearing a smart pair of blue striped pyjamas the lad was listening through his headphones to the hospital radio. She approached his bed and he took off the headphones and looked at her directly. 'I didn't die' he said.

'No but we nearly did, you gave us all such a fright. Please don't do it again Norman.' He feigned repentance and then looked serious just for a moment. He was well aware how much concern there had been about him. 'Thanks to all of you I'm still here.'

'And don't we know it' she laughed as he picked up his headphones again and at full blast listened to Guy Mitchell singing 'She wears red feathers and a hula hula skirt.'

'The ward changes are up' Margaret and Julie were in the kitchen clearing their respective trolleys. For the moment their experience on the surgical ward was ending, time to move to another department. 'Where are we going?'

'I'm on men's medical, they say Sister Lester's a terror.'

'Am I on there as well.'

Just as it Was

'No you're down to work in out-patients' Julie breathed a sigh of relief. She knew full well of Sister Lester's reputation and she didn't envy her friend who was going to work on her ward. 'I'm sure that she'll have no grumbles with you I think that the rest of the staff on there are good.' All the same she was pleased that her move was to outpatients. There was drama and variety and so many different demands made on the nursing and medical staff in that department and she looked forward to it.

Just as it Was

10

Accident and Emergency

Julie awoke to a bedroom full of sunlight. She looked up and followed the lines made by the cracks in the whitewashed ceiling. Following the well known rises and falls which had become as familiar to her as her own face in the mirror this was the room that she had shared with her sisters and today was Bab's wedding day. The reception was to be held at home and where was everybody. Yesterday had been a hectic day in the accident and emergency department and she must have slept in. The bedroom door was pushed open 'here you are' Doris was handing her a cup of tea 'we left you because you were fast on but you'll have to get a move on now. The bathroom's free so don't mess about you've only got an hour before you leave for church and Babs has to come in here to put her dress on.' Julie sat up 'thanks Doris, I can't believe that Babs is going to leave us, it's going to be so different without her.'

'I expect we'll all leave one day, come on don't get broody about it drink your tea.' Time moved quickly and after a quick bath and grabbing a sandwich Julie was in the thick of the melee. Mrs Spencer was trying to get things done and was beginning to panic.'Mum don't get into a state,' there was about half an hour to go before the wedding car was due to

Just as it Was

arrive to take the bridal party to the church. 'I haven't got the table set yet and there's people knocking on the door every few minutes.' Doris and Mum with the help of a neighbour were putting out the wedding feast in the living room. Jellies and trifles and tins of salmon and boiled ham had been got together from the food rations and friends and relatives had helped out to provide the buffet. A wedding cake, which had been iced with much care and detail by Mrs Scott who lived in the next street had been proudly delivered last night to the admiration of all who saw it and it was now standing precariously on the table in the passageway, the place was in an uproar. Julie was going to change into her bridesmaid dress Babs looked at her sister as she came through the door. 'Julie where've you been? You'll never be ready in time'.

'Don't worry Babs, everything'll turn out all right, don't panic it's your wedding day, let the others do the worrying and just make yourself beautiful for Derek.' Julie took off her dressing gown and slipped on the long silk dress which had been borrowed from a cousin, and after fixing on her floral headdress she was ready for the church. She helped Babs to fix her veil taking care not to disturb her sister's hair and make up. 'You look gorgeous,' she bent and kissed Babs on the cheek, she was going to miss her and tears were close. 'The flowers have arrived and we're just about ready. I think the car's here for us,' The voice of their mother came from the bottom of the stairs, 'the car's here come on' and as Julie went down and looked at her Mum she saw her chin quiver and a tear in her eye. 'I'll see you in church then,' Mrs Spencer and Doris along with Freda and Harry were driven off

Just as it Was

leaving Babs Mr Spencer and Julie waiting for their car. Julie saw her father's eye watering. Weddings were supposed to be happy occasions but Babs was leaving them to marry and set up home somewhere else with her new husband and the family unit was changing.

'I'm going to be late for work.' After the celebrations of yesterday the house was full of slumbering relatives from Lancashire as evidenced by the gentle snores coming from Harry and Freda's room. Rosie from next door had put up Mrs Spencer's sister Ethel and her husband Charlie. Doncaster relatives had helped out with sleeping arrangements for cousins and friends from afar and now Julie was finding her way through the debris of the day before. She tried not to disturb the others finding it difficult. The living room looked exhausted with a disarray of clothes thrown over the backs of chairs, a result of the overflow of extra people in the house. Glasses and plates left here and there would all be greeting her mother who would be busy again today and she wished that she could have been there to help and to see more of her Aunts and Uncles but duty called and she would have to wait until she came off duty tonight before she saw them again.

The staff in the accident and emergency department was down to a minimum at the weekends, today Julie was on duty with Brody a junior sister. The casualty officer was on call and in his absence one of the other doctors filled in. There were no clinics or dressings and Julie hoped that it wouldn't be too

Just as it Was

hectic. There were likely to be a few people turning up, usually foreign bodies in eyes, some who had fallen and hurt themselves, and perhaps a youngster or two who had shot up a temperature or developed a tummy ache that wouldn't go away. In the case of an influx of patients staff would be taken from a ward where they could be spared, and most of the nurses enjoyed the experience of working there amidst the chaos, which was sometimes accident and emergency. Today Julie was checking the stock and the trolleys to make sure that they were ready for all emergencies when the phone rang. 'We've a road accident, the ambulance has just arrived, a twenty year old female with multiple injuries and a male who is unconscious.' Just for a moment a wave of panic swept over her but in a second she gathered herself and told herself that she was now a second year nurse and although her experience in A&E had been short she had Sister Brody there. 'Dr Gibson has been informed and he's on his way,' the porter in the A&E reception had passed the details on to the nursing staff and Julie fetched the trolley as Sister Brody checked the oxygen and the drugs cupboard and splints. They had everything ready as Joe wheeled in the woman, 'Nurse Spencer can you look after this patient until the Dr arrives, I'm going to ring the ward for another nurse, we're going to need more help down here.' Julie approached the young woman who was tearful and anxious and obviously distressed. 'Hello, what's your name?'

'I'm Mary, Mary Smithurst, oh please how's my boy friend?'

'The doctor's just arrived and he's examining him now, I'll let you know as soon as I get to know anything, but what about

Just as it Was

you?' she cast a professional eye over the young woman who seemed to be fully aware. 'I think that I was lucky, the other car hit the driver's side head on, I've got a few bruises and cuts but I'm more worried about Phil.'

'I'll find out what I can after the Dr examines him, he'll need to examine you as well.' After a brief look at the girl to assure herself that she could be safely left for a few minutes Julie said reassuringly 'just you lie still and I'll go and see what's happening.' Dr Gibson and Sister Brody were behind the curtains in one of the cubicles attending to the injured man when Julie quietly peeped in to ask how things were. They looked up as Julie asked about him he was beginning to moan and show signs of recovering consciousness, attempting to speak' Julie spoke quietly to Dr Gibson 'Mary his girlfriend wants to know how he is' she whispered. 'I'll come and have a word with her, I've done what I can for him at the moment' Dr Gibson moved towards Julie and they walked together towards the cubicle where the girl lay. 'How are you?' he smiled sympathetically at Mary.

'I don't think I'm too bad just a bit bruised but I'm worried about Phil.'

'Well he's going to be admitted after we've X-rayed him, and when we get the results of the X-rays we'll know more. He is beginning to try to talk to us so that's a good sign. Now, shall I have a look at you?' After examining her carefully taking her blood pressure and observing her breathing and pulse rate Dr Gibson asked Nurse Spencer to dress the woman's abrasions and help her into a wheelchair. 'We're going to find a bed for your boyfriend,' he turned to Sister Brody who had joined

Just as it Was

them after leaving Phil in the care of Nurse Johnson who had been sent down from one of the wards. 'Can you do that please Sister?' Turning back to the girl he said, 'as soon as he's settled on the ward you can go to see him. If that's all I'll go and do the paperwork , the radiographer should be in soon to do those X-rays.' Julie wheeled the dressing trolley into the cubicle and set about cleaning and dressing Mary's wounds. The girl seemed easier more settled now 'he's dishy, a real bedside manner.'

'Who Dr Gibson? I don't know much about him I suppose he is quite as you say dishy, but hey what about your Phil?'

'Oh that's different.'

'Well that's you nicely bandaged up, I'll go and find a wheelchair and ask the porter to take you along with Phil when he goes up to X-ray.' The phone was ringing again Sister Brody looked at Julie, 'what now? it looks like being quite a session.'

'We have a young girl on her way here, severe abdominal pain' the porter's voice echoed out over the phone. 'Will you admit her nurse?' Sister Brody asked Julie as the ambulance bell was heard ringing out as it came down the drive and pulled up outside A&E. 'I'll contact Dr Gibson.' The porter wheeled in a trolley bearing a girl of about ten years old who was accompanied by her Mum. 'Put her in this cubicle' the girl was obviously in a great deal of pain and as Julie took her details she assured the Mum that the doctor would soon be there to examine her daughter. Very soon Dr Gibson came back stethoscope hanging from his neck looking very

Just as it Was

handsome, professional and rather windswept. 'Phew there's no let up this morning I've sorted out the man injured in the car accident he's in X-ray at the moment and there's a bed for him on ward four. What have you got for me now?' the young doctor seemed to be enjoying his role as casualty officer in the absence of his colleague. 'A young girl with abdominal pain her name's Beth,' with Julie accompanying him he examined the girl carefully. She winced as he gently pressed on her abdomen.' Tenderness in the right iliac fossa nurse (the lower right side of the abdomen.) now what could that be; appendix? Well young lady I think I'll ask your Mum to come back in here and we can find out a bit more about this.' Beth's mum anxiously went up to her daughter. 'What's going to happen Dr?'

'I better get the R.S.O. (resident surgical officer.) to have a look at her Mrs Taylor, he turned and walked towards the exit 'I think that she may need surgery,' he spoke quietly to the mother to avoid the girl hearing. 'I'll go and get in touch with him.' Julie looked at the youngster who was pale and tearful, she took her hand. 'We'll make you better we've got some very nice doctors and nurses here who will find out what's wrong with your tummy and then we'll put it right, you want to get rid of that nasty old pain don't you?' Beth nodded her head. 'Right well the doctor will soon be here so until then I'll leave your Mum and you together is that O.K.?' Beth was turning a definite pucy colour, 'nurse I feel sick' she said and Julie just managed to make it in time with the vomit bowl.

The R.S.O arrived quite quickly and decided that the best thing to do was to admit Beth for observation. 'Another

Just as it Was

patient for you, this time a young girl with abdominal pain.' Julie spoke to the staff nurse on ward three, whose urgency week it was. 'Is it the light that's attracting them, you seem to be pretty busy down there' the staff nurse cracked a joke. In fact the patients continued to arrive and the minute Dr Gibson left to go to his quarters he was summoned back to casualty. There was a string of minor accidents, a lady had let the tin opener slip and gashed her hand and that required stitching and a tetanus injection, an F.B. (foreign body) in eye required drops after which Dr Gibson successfully removed it, and a man scalded himself with a kettle whilst making a cup of tea for his wife. 'It's the first and last time that I'll let him do that' said the wife who had accompanied him and was put out by the disturbance to her Sunday afternoon. Gradually things quietened down and the shift was coming to an end. Dr was completing his form filling and as Sister Brody and Julie filled in their report and cleaned up the trolleys and the cubicles there was just time for a cup of tea before they finally left. 'Would you like a drink Dr Gibson?'

'Thanks that would be very welcome' he walked into the office and sat on the edge of the desk. 'Well, that was an experience, you never know what's going to happen in A&E.'

'For a Sunday it's been quite interesting, it can be a bit quiet sometimes.'

'Well it's been a pleasure working with you two.' (Nurse Johnson had gone back to her ward earlier in the afternoon.) 'You'll be going over to the nurses home to get your feet up now I expect.'

Just as it Was

'Not me I live out.' Julie rinsed her cup in the sink and wiping it placed it back into the cupboard.

'Oh well let's hope that we work together again sometime.'

'You never know' Sister Brody said and entered into a discussion with Dr Gibson asking him about how he had felt working in A/E. The two continued to talk about the happenings of the afternoon, Dr Gibson seemed reluctant to go. Julie felt anxious to get back home where the family would still be in celebration mood and so she said goodbye and went to catch her bus back to Wysten.

When she reached home she found her parents alone in the living room. The relatives had gone off to visit other kin and Mr and Mrs Spencer were taking it easy after all the extra work of the wedding. Julie's mother handed her a letter 'this came for you yesterday and I forgot to tell you with all the excitement of the wedding, it's from London.' Julie picked up the letter examining the unfamiliar handwriting, the postmark was Battersea. 'Oh heavens I think that I know who this is from, it'll be from Jane Rolands. 'Who's she?'

'Don't you remember me telling you about Jane Mum, she lost a leg in the train disaster. She sent me a card last Christmas and she said that she'd write. I wonder what she wants.' 'Well open it and find out.' Jenny eagerly ripped open the envelope and quickly read the short letter.

Dear Nurse Spencer.

It has taken me some time to get used to walking about on my artificial leg, but at last I am making some headway. I can go out to the park now and I went shopping with my mother

Just as it Was

last week. Everyone has been so helpful and I am feeling a lot more cheerful than I did at first. There are a lot of things that I cant do but I am thankful to still be here after the awful crash. My family will never forget the hospital and all that everyone there did for us. You and me became such good friends and if you remember I said that I would like you to come to London and stay with us. Well I think that if you could come perhaps next Spring I will be ready to go out and about and show you the sights of London. What do you think? I do hope that you say yes, it would mean such a lot to me. Let me know as soon as you can.

Very best wishes, Your friend Jane

Julie read out the letter to her mother and her father listened as it registered on him what was being said.

'What do you think Mum?'

'London's a lovely place, your Dad and I've been a couple of times.'

Mr Spencer sucked on his pipe. 'You're too young your only just eighteen, London's full of spivs and sharpsters, and we don't know these people at all.'

'I know them Dad, they're lovely people, Jane will be so upset if I say I can't go.'

'I'm sorry, perhaps when you're a bit older but it's far too big and far too busy, you're not going all that way on your own 'til your older. Write and tell your friend you can't go just now, her parents 'll understand.' Julie started to object.

Just as it Was

'That's enough now, you've heard what your father's said, you can go when you're a bit older.' Her mother gave the final word and Julie stomped angrily out of the room.

Just as it Was

11

The Prowler

After working in outpatients Julie was moved to a medical ward. She met up with Margaret Williams again, the girl whom she had shared a room with in P.T.S, the two girls were walking back from the dispensary together. 'How do you like being on a medical ward?' the other girl asked her.

'It's a bit tame after surgery and outpatients; I liked the excitement and drama there. It's all nursing care and medicines there's so many older patients as well, heart problems, bronchitis, it makes you dread getting old.'

Margaret laughed 'we've a long way to go yet before we're old, let's enjoy ourselves first, how's Colin by the way?'

'We still write but it's not easy to see much of each other, he's got plans about what he wants to do when he comes out of the army.'

'What are they?'

'He wants to emigrate to Canada and he wants me to go with him.'

'That sounds exciting what did you say?'

'Well I wont have finished my training by then, I haven't decided yet and it's a bit early in our relationship.'

Just as it Was

'What do your Mum and Dad say?'

'I haven't mentioned it to them, I don't think that they'll be very pleased about the idea though they both like Colin, but I mean Canada it's a long way to go.'

'How much longer has he got in the army?'

'About a year I think, to tell you the truth since he mentioned it I haven't thought much about it.'

'I'm not being nosey but how do you really feel about Colin, you've been going out with him for quite a while now it's a big step to think about going all that way?'

'I was crackers about him when I first met him' she hesitated, ' I'm not sure, we don't see all that much of each other what with him in the army and me working all sorts of funny hours even when he does get home on leave. His letters keep coming regularly and he's quite keen on us staying together. I've really been too busy to think about the future.'

'It's not much fun for you though him being so far away, I think that you ought to get out and about a bit more.'

'Margaret, I think that you should open up an agony aunt's advice page I've known Colin for a long time now and I'm not bothered about going out with anybody else.' They had reached the floor where they both worked. 'You don't know what you're missing, there's more to life than nursing.'

'Well I don't know about that' the girls parted to return to to their own ward, 'see you at the lecture tomorrow, and remember we've both got to get through our nursing exams yet.'

Just as it Was

The few months on the medical ward passed slowly. Sister Hardy was a hard taskmaster and she kept an eagle on her nurses. Julie was glad when the time came for her to move on and she was now down for a spell of night duty on the male orthopaedic ward. The long building was apart from the main hospital it was reached by walking along the concreted pathway, which was covered by a roof of convoluted tin sheeting supported by wooden spars. The nurses pulled their cloaks tightly around themselves as they went on duty in winter and they were pleased to reach the warm interior. The coke stoves, which were set in a line down the centre of the ward, gave off a cosy heat. A long row of beds ran down each side of the ward and the paraphernalia of splints, weights, hand-grips, all testament to the injuries that the patients had met with were a damning picture of their work in the coal-mines. Not all were miners; there were road traffic accidents, motorbikes in particular and also patients with diseases of the bone. The nurse's work was heavy, a lot of lifting was involved but usually the ward was a cheerful one with a lot of banter between the resilient patients and the staff. Mr Chalmers a forty something year old patient had a spinal injury and a fractured femur. He was in a plaster cast and as he needed traction for the leg he was also encased in an adapted Thomas's splint. 'You poor man' the nurses sympathised with him but he would have none of it. 'What! with all you beauties looking after me, I'm the luckiest man alive and I'll walk out of here in a few months time, you see if I don't'. The miner's spirit was full of energy and his attitude

Just as it Was

was typical of most of the men on the ward. They had a good regard for the nurses and when any one of them had her two nights off duty the men clubbed together and insisted that she should take the money and treat herself to the pictures. The nurses did this reluctantly but the men wouldn't hear of any of them refusing. It was a good ward to be on and Julie enjoyed the teasing that they cheerfully put up with from the men. The hot drinks had been given and as Nurse Jessop, the senior nurse gave out the medicines she reached Mr Chalmer's bed. 'How are you tonight, you look as though you're in pain?'

'Staff nurse gave me two codeine tablets earlier but they haven't done much good.'

'Why didn't you say something to her?'

'They were so busy nurse, I didn't want to bother them.'

'Well Dr Gibson will be coming to do his night round soon, I'll ask him to write you up for something stronger.' The two nurses finished their care of the rest of the ward and they now sat at the table as they took out the report book to have a closer look at the new admissions. It had been a busy day on the ward and they hoped that the new patients, a fourteen-year-old boy who had fallen off his bike and broken his leg and an elderly man who had fallen and sustained a fractured femur would settle down comfortably.

'Night Sister will be round soon.'

'I hope that she comes early, poor Mr Shaw woke with a start last night when she shone her torch on his face to see if he

Just as it Was

was still breathing, it took him ages to get off to sleep again, he wasn't very pleased with her.'

'I shouldn't think he was pleased, fancy being woken up like that.' The girls sat at the table and chatted quietly as gentle snores began to sound around them.' 'The senior nurse was an avid admirer of Burt Lancaster and she began to tell Julie of the film and adventurous roll that she had seen recently which starred him. She was also very particular about her own appearance and Julie had to put up with long winded stories about how she polished up her 'beetle crushes' and she held them up for Julie to inspect. 'Very nice, I think that I better put my best foot forward and go and fill the coke hods, I'll just put my cloak on.'

'Take care out there, there's been talk of a prowler in the hospital grounds.'

Julie looked questioningly at Nurse Jessop, 'who by?'

'Nurse Dennis she told me the other day, her bedroom's on the ground floor near the bike shed. She very kindly arranged to leave her window slightly open from time to time for a couple of third year nurses to climb through after a late night out. One night she was sat up in bed reading before going to sleep when Nurse Simpson from the next bedroom popped in and told her that she thought she'd heard a foot step outside and asked if she'd heard anything, Dennis went over to the window and looked out, and couldn't see anyone and she said that she thought that perhaps it might be a stray cat. Simpson told her to shut her window just in case, she said that she couldn't because she'd promised to leave it open for

Just as it Was

Chambers and Cliff so Simpson went off and Dennis picked her book up again and was reading when she heard a noise outside her window. She was frightened to death and jumped out of bed ran upstairs and got into bed with her friend Hartley. Well you know how big Hartley is; she objected loudly there wasn't much room but Dennis was so frightened she refused to go back to her own room, she wouldn't get out of the bed. Hartley was trying to push her out and there she was snivelling and crying and saying she was scared. They must have had a very uncomfortable night two big girls like them I bet they didn't get much sleep.' Julie was trying to stifle her laughter at the picture of the two lying side by side in the single bed the resentful Simpson and the frightened Dennis neither of them was sylphlike and she wondered if their friendship had survived such an episode. Julie listened to the tale and then said 'Do you think there is a prowler? I'll be careful and keep my eyes open.' Picking up the hods she made for the door 'whoops' as she reached the door it flung open and Dr Gibson came through. ''Good Heavens, I'm so sorry I seem to have a habit of bumping into you.'

Julie blushed, 'Oh yes that day in outpatients.'

'What are you doing?'

'I'm on my way to fill these' she held up one of the coke hods.

'That's a man's job, give them here I'll do that' he smiled at her encouragingly.

'But I'll get into trouble it's my job the junior nurse always fills them.'

Just as it Was

Nurse Jessop appeared from the ward 'what's happening? oh it's you Dr Gibson I thought that it might be the prowler.'

'What! what prowler?, no I've come to see if any of the patients need anything but first I'm going to fill these coke hods for nurse Spencer, especially if as you say there's a prowler about it's very dark out there.'

Julie was embarrassed, 'well then you better come back into the ward nurse Spencer and without another word Nurse Jessop returned to the ward. When he came back in carrying the coke hods Dr Gibson washed his hands and after looking at the two new patients and talking to Mr Chalmers about his pain he gave instructions for stronger medication. 'I'll hang on here for a bit to see if Mr Chalmers feels more comfortable.' They moved into the ward office to do the writing up, when he'd finished Dr asked 'what's this about a prowler?'

'I'll get nurse Spencer to tell you, I promised earlier to go and sit with young Tommy who fell off his cycle today, he's a young lad on a men's ward and he's a bit homesick. Nurse Spencer make Dr Gibson a cup of tea and take it to him in the office.' Julie went into the kitchen and made the tea and then she took it through to the doctor. She smiled nervously as she handed Dr Gibson his tea 'thank you' he said, 'now are you going to tell me about this prowler?' Hesitantly Julie outlined the story skipping the bits, which she felt, were unsuitable; she just recounted the bare bones. 'Hmmn! I wonder what's going on we'll have to take care.'

'Have you finished your tea Dr Gibson, I'll take your cup.' The young nurse felt uncomfortable at being left alone with the Dr.

Just as it Was

'Thank you nurse, I enjoyed that, I'll just check up on Mr Chalmers and then I'll be on my way.'

'Right Nurse Spencer, Mr Jones needs to be lifted up the bed and made more comfortable, I'd like you to give me a hand.' The rest of the patients were settled down but Mr Jones was always slipping down the bed and with his chronic bronchitis there was a chance of him developing other chest problems, therefore the nurses were always hoicking him up the bed. 'What would I do without you girls, you're little angels you are.' Mr Jones reached under his pillow and brought out a bag of sweets, 'here you are, take these, my wife'll be bringing me some more tomorrow.'

'We can't take your sweets, it's very nice of you but we just can't.'

'Give over, I'd give you more than sweets if I could, all you do for us, be good girls and take 'em.'

'Thank you' she looked at the sweets 'ooh these are my favourites' Nurse Jessop smiled at him sweetly, 'thank you, when the patients are like you it's the best job in the world.' Eventually the ward was quiet and as the two nurses sat at the table Nurse Jessop said to Julie you're getting well into your training now are you enjoying it?'

'It's fine, I am, but we've got a lecture tomorrow at nine thirty, I think I'll be falling asleep I've got to go though with the prelims coming up I can't afford to miss any of the lectures.'

'Afraid so, it's something that we all have to put up with, if you like we can do a bit of revision now, she looked at Julie

Just as it Was

questioningly what shall I ask you let me think, how about telling me how you would set up a trolley for a lumbar puncture.' The girls became engrossed in the revision until a voice sounded from halfway down the ward, 'nurse can I have a bottle please?'

Handing over to the day staff next morning Nurse Jessop and Nurse Spencer made their way to the dining room for breakfast. By the time that she had eaten Julie blearily made her way to the Badminton Hall where the lecture was to take place. In a few weeks time she would be taking the preliminary part of the state exam and she thought to herself how quickly the time had gone since she started her nursing career. In just over another two years she would be taking her finals and then what? she wondered. Colin was coming home this weekend, he still mentioned going to Canada when he wrote to her but did he really intend to go? How could she even think about it with the rest of her training to do, they would have to discuss it when they saw each other again. For the moment she just wanted to get the lecture over with, catch the next bus home roll into bed and have a good sleep ready to go on duty again tonight.

'Julie it's time you were getting ready to go to the hospital.' Mrs Spencer called up the stairs to her daughter who had promptly washed her face brushed her hair and tumbled into bed on reaching home. Now it was time to go back on duty, it was the third night of her five night duty rota and she was looking forward to having her two nights off and a chance to spend some time with her boyfriend. Since he had last been

Just as it Was

on a short weekend leave so much had happened in her career. Nursing and the new relationships that she had made with the other nurses seemed to fill her life completely. The long hours that she spent on duty at the hospital and attending the lectures, and also travelling from home and back again meant that she often left home early in the morning and arrived home when the day was over, it was well past half past nine at night when she arrived there. Now I'm on night duty I'll be grumpy because it takes me till the second day of my nights off before I feel human, I hope that Colin can put up with it. She thought of Mr Chalmers who had said to her 'now then sleepyhead head how are you?' when she had taken a bottle to him at five in the morning. Night duty was a world apart from the rest of humanity and the four a clock zenith was the mountain she and most of her colleagues, had to climb.

Julie and Nurse Jessop walked over to the orthopaedic ward together after changing into their caps and aprons in the cloakroom of the main hospital block. 'How did the lecture go?'

'Oh I managed to stay awake and take some notes it was Miss Weaver giving a lecture on diseases of the uterus. Just what you need after a night on an orthopaedic ward.'

'Have you worked on the gynae ward (gynaecological ward.)?'

'No I've got that to look forward to, at the moment I'm quite happy where I am the patients on this ward are super.'

Just as it Was

'We've had a pretty quiet time of it so far, let's hope that it continues. 'The pattern followed that of the previous nights, the ward was settling down and and the lights were dimmed as Julie collected in the remaining bottles and took them into the sluice. She thought about her next task and putting on her cloak she was ready to go outside and fill up the coke hods. As she opened up the door and left the comfort of the ward with it's heaving humanity behind the emptiness and the blackness of the night struck her. The bunker lay at the side of the building between that and the next ward and the eerie darkness caused her to shiver. It was necessary to go between the two buildings in order to fill the hods and she felt nervous as she recalled the story of the prowler. There were two hods and after filling the first one she prepared to carry it back inside. As she turned to go back she looked up to the road which ran alongside the hospital and she was alarmed to see a dark figure moving furtively through the bushes which edged the path. As fast as she could she picked up the hod and hurried through the door of the ward. Nurse Jessop was in the sluice filling up the sterilizer in case it was needed during the night. 'Nurse Jessop,' she caught her breath, 'there's someone in the hospital grounds, I've just seen someone prowling around in the bushes.' Julie was trembling and pleased to be back in the safety of the ward.'Oh my goodness, are you sure Nurse Spencer, let's go and have another look.' She took her cloak and as they opened the door the two could see a figure in the distance. 'I'll ring the porters lodge, Joe Biggs is on duty tonight.'

Just as it Was

Julie was eager to get help but she asked 'will he be able to do anything, he's nearly ready to retire and he's just got back to work after hip surgery?'

'He's all we've got Julie' with that the senior nurse went off to ring the porter. 'Joe was a short rather overweight man and the thought of him tackling an intruder seemed a bit of a long shot to both the girls but in no time at all Joe arrived as the nurses waited for him anxiously. They had taken it in turns to keep an eye on the situation and the prowler was still in their sights. 'I've spotted 'im, I've spotted 'im' Joe babbled excitedly, 'quick give me something heavy he's coming towards us.' Julie ran into the ward and grabbed the heaviest thing that she could see which happened to be the pole for opening the windows. Joe grabbed it, the pole was at least twice as high as him and it was waving about dangerously as he stood on the edge of the path looking towards the road. By this time the three of them were nervously and excitedly wondering what to do next. 'Ring for the police,' Joe called as he bravely advanced towards the figure, pole wobbling precariously.'Hang on' he came to a sudden stop, 'I think that I know who it is'

As the figure got closer the three recognised Dr Gibson. 'What on earth are you doing with that pole Joe?' he asked. 'You look like Little John crossing the ford.'

'We thought you were the prowler, we were just about to ring the police.'

Dr Gibson laughed, 'I was looking for him, I heard the rumours and I thought that I'd have a scout around there's

Just as it Was

nobody about tonight.' Julie felt relief, but what was the doctor doing why was he taking on the search. It seemed very odd to her but perhaps he really thought that the night staff were in danger, if that were so then why? she thought that it was an extraordinary thing for him to do.

'Dr Gibson come and have a cup of tea in the kitchen I think we've all had enough excitement for one night, and you better have one too Joe.'

'Thank you' Dr Gibson followed the group into the corridor. 'I've actually come to do my night round, it all looks very peaceful in here.'

'I'll just take a look at the patients to see if everyone's alright, you put the kettle on nurse Spencer.' The ward door opened and Night Sister came in. She looked surprised to see the group 'is there a problem, what are you doing here Joe?'

'I rang for Joe sister, we thought that we saw the prowler but it was a false alarm.'

'Oh the prowler, the police have been called in and all boyfriends have been banned from the hospital grounds, you'll be hearing all about it tomorrow they have to wait at the gate

Just as it Was

12

Colin On Leave

Margaret Williams giggled as her boyfriend pulled her towards himself and kissed her. 'You're going to have to be careful, they've called the police in about the prowler, boyfriends have been banned from the hospital grounds.'

'Not this one, they can't keep me away from you.'

'Brian, hush don't let anyone know you're here, you're as mad as a hatter.'

'We haven't been caught yet have we?'

'No but home sister will be doing her round soon you better leave before she gets here.'

Brian gave her another kiss and went towards the door to leave. 'Oh my God,' he ducked back into the room, 'she's out there she's just gone into Nurse Hartley's room.'

'She's early tonight what shall we do, I know, quick hide in the linen room it's three doors up on the other side of the corridor.' Brian made a dash across the deserted space as Margaret popped back into her own room and made a pretence of getting ready for bed as she waited for sister to arrive. Suddenly she heard a scream looking out onto the corridor she saw Nurse Jones emerging from the bathroom in a cloud of steam, she was dashing to her room trying to hide

Just as it Was

her modesty as she had jumped out of the bath when a man had entered the bathroom. Brian came out of the bathroom desperately trying to escape. Home sister emerged from the bedroom where she had been talking to the nurse. In a panic Brian ran into her knocking her flying down she went flat on her back with her feet up in the air showing all she'd got, suspenders holding up her her black stockings and Marks and Spencer's pink bloomers (winter warmers) which were chosen to keep out the cold when walking across the straight mile to the hospital were on full view to all and sundry. 'It's the prowler, it's the prowler,' Chris Walker was the first out of her room and in her baggy teddy bear pyjamas she ran towards the staircase. 'I'm going to ring the police he's knocked home sister down.'

Nurse Williams called out 'don't, stop it, please, it's my boyfriend.' Heads popped out of bedroom doors as girls some in flannelette nighties and others who were more racily clad in skimpy negligees which exposed bare expanses of bosom and leg all swarmed towards Brian. At another time it would have been a dream come true but now he wished never again to enter a nurses' home. He leaned over the dazed home sister and tried to help her to her feet, perhaps he could redeem himself. She was beginning to look around 'where am I what happened,' she asked groggily.

One of the more senior nurses pushed forward and knelt down beside the bewildered sister. 'Are you alright Sister, can you get up.'

'What an earth has happened, somebody ran into me I heard a lot of screaming and shouting and saw lots of people in

Just as it Was

pyjamas.' She looked around slowly getting her bearings, her gaze focussed on Brian Crookes. 'Who are you young man?'

'I'm Brian I was just visiting my friend Nurse Williams, I accidentally ran into you I'm sorry if I hurt you.'

'Why were you running along the corridor what were you doing in here?'

'I wasn't doing any harm, I didn't mean to hurt you.'

'You shouldn't be here,' her senses were returning and she gathered herself as she shakily struggled to her feet. 'We don't allow men up here.' Brian couldn't think of anything to say he was caught red handed.

'I'll have to report this matter to matron tomorrow you and Nurse Williams will be hearing more about it we can't have this sort of thing going on. Now then you better leave this building, I don't know how you got in, but Nurse Hartley will let you out with this key. She handed the key to Hartley 'will someone make me a cup of tea please, I'd like to sit down for a little while until I recover.'

The next day Julie was sorry to hear about the dismissal of Margaret Williams. Of the twenty or so girls who had been with her in P.T.S more then half had left. Some had gone to Matron with sound reasons for leaving while others had done a moonlight flit. Margaret had chosen to live in after P.T.S. no doubt wishing to leave behind the restrictions of home but she had been foolish and had to pay the price. It had not been wise letting her boyfriend into her room whatever the reason and scandal would not be tolerated.

Just as it Was

Eva Spencer picked up the letters from the doormat, there was one from London, postmarked Battersea. Julie had been writing to Jane roughly about once a month and her mother knew that she nursed a strong wish to visit the girl in London. Julie was a good eighteen years old now and her father would perhaps be more inclined to let her go. Babs and Doris were both married and they had broken down a lot of the barriers for their younger sister. It was nineteen fifty and the post war era had seen more freedom and prosperity for all age groups compared to the pre-war era. London was an exciting place the theatres and restaurants and the shops were getting back to full strength and fashion was flaunting the busy streets of the capital. Regent Street and Oxford Street which. were full of the buoyant life sweeping through the capital were featured regularly in the magazines which Julie occasionally bought. She walked into the living room stifling a yawn, 'I heard the post through the letter box Mum.'

'Yes there's two for you, one from London and one from Richmond.'

'That'll be Colin and Jane' Julie took the letters from her mother who went through into the kitchen to fill the kettle before putting it on the coal fire. When she came back her daughter was reading the letters, Mrs Spencer took cups from the kitchen cupboard and from the cellar head she produced bread and proceeded to slice and toast it at the fire after letting down the front bar. 'Any news?' she asked.

Just as it Was

'Colin wont be home until tomorrow, there's a special parade and the whole platoon has to be present. That means we'll only have Sunday together.'

'And what about the other one, the letter from London?'

'Jane is asking me to go and stay later in the year, I've saved a bit of money, do you think Dad'll let me go?'

'I'll have a word, we'll have to wait and see what he says. You'll be able to catch up with yourself with Colin not coming home 'til Sunday. That bedroom of yours needs sorting out.'

'I haven't had much time mum, what with working on nights and trying to swat for my prelims I've been too busy for anything else.'

'Well there's not much time it's true, you seem to spend all your life going backwards and forwards to the hospital. It's not just a job it takes everything else over.'

'I'll be coming off nights soon and I take the exam in a couple of weeks, things 'll be better after that. Perhaps I could go to London next year when the better weather arrives.'

'We'll see what your Dad says, what are you and Colin doing on Sunday?'

'I expect we'll go for a walk, there's not much to do on Sundays.'

'Well if he wants to come and have his dinner with us he's welcome.'

'Oh thanks Mum, I'll ask him as soon as I see him.'

Just as it Was

'Come on let's get these pots washed then you can tidy your bedroom while I do that bit of ironing.'

The train was on time and as Julie waited at the top of the station steps she waved as Colin came into sight. A neighbour had offered her a lift in his little Ford as he had business in town and he was now waiting to take the couple back to Wysten. In the back of the car Colin put his arm around her, 'it's good to see you again, I wish that I didn't have to go back.'

'I know Colin but lets make the most of it now you're here. She kissed his cheek and whispered, 'Mum's invited you to have dinner with us, would you like to come?'

'Course I would, and I want to talk to you about what we're going to do.'

'I'm sure we'll get a chance I expect that they'll fall asleep after dinner. Dad always goes to bed Sunday afternoon after he's been to the pub and eaten and I think John's got a date with a new girl friend.' The car was pulled to a stop as the driver applied the brakes at the top of the street where Colin lived. 'Here we are, I'll drop you off first Colin.'

'Thanks for the lift ,it's good of you, any time I can do you a favour,' he turned to Julie 'what time shall I come round Julie?'

'About twelve, we'll have time for a chat before dinner then.'

Just as it Was

Colin arrived promptly and as Julie answered the front door they hung his coat up in the passage and snatched a brief kiss before Dad appeared, 'Hello lad, how's life in the army then?'

'Hello Mr Spencer, it's not too bad but I'll be glad when I've finished, it's a long way from home.'

'Well at least there's not a war on.'

'Some of the lads are signing on after their Z reserve's up. they might get sent to war.' Things don't look too good in Korea.'

'You're right there there'll always be fighting somewhere.'

'Come through to where it's warm don't stand in the passage talking.' Mrs Spencer called through to them from the living room as she was mixing the Yorkshire puddings.

'I'm just going for a pint before me dinner, you can with me if you like lad.'

'That would be nice Mr Spencer.' Julie looked dumbfounded.

'Me and Colin have things to talk about Dad.'

''We wont be long, you two can talk after dinner' and the two men walked off up the street together towards the local pub after Colin squeezed her hand and promised to be back soon.

'Mum what's Dad thinking of, Colin's only here for the day, he's got to be back in camp by midday tomorrow.'

'You know what men are like, I suppose he didn't want to disappoint your dad, they'll be back before you know it.'

Julie wasn't too sure about that, she remembered the numerous times when Sunday dinner had been ready to be

Just as it Was

put out on the plates and her father was still at the pub. She and her mother however got on with the cooking, it was leg of lamb as usual. The menu never changed, roast lamb Sunday, cold lamb and veg on Monday, and Hash on Tuesday. A huge rice pudding was put in the bottom of the side oven as the meat was cooking and this was served up for afters as long as it lasted.

'They wont be long now, the meats done, I'll put the vegetables on to boil and we can get the table set.'

'Have you mentioned my London trip to Dad?'

'We have been talking about it, London's a big place with a lot of funny things going on.'

'But I'm staying with Jane and her family Mum, nothings going to happen to me.'

'I think your dads in the same mind as me, you're old enough to know your own mind now if you want to go, you go.'

'That's great, thanks Mum, I'll write to Battersea and let them know, we can make some arrangements then.'

'I'd better get these potatoes mashed, the men 'll be back any-time.'

'Crickey I didn't realise it was quarter past one, where are they?'

As the minutes ticked by Mrs Spencer became more and more put out. Julie heard the old signs of annoyance as the pan lids were put down on the kitchen sink with a clatter, and when she came through to the living room her mother was tight lipped, and impatient. 'It's always the same, when he gets to

Just as it Was

the pub he never knows what time to come home. I thought it'd be different with Colin being with him.' Julies insides began to churn, she remembered similar occasions when she was much younger and many a dinner had been dried to a cinder. When her father had eventually returned home accusations were hurled and an almighty row followed. Sometimes it even led to Eva Spencer packing her bags and walking out of the door with Julie and John when they were small. 'Don't get upset Mum, if you like we can have our dinner and put theirs on plates.'

In truth Julie was very upset herself, she had looked forward to Colin's visit and although she realised that it would have been hard for him to refuse her father's invitation to go to the pub with him she had expected them to return home in a reasonable time for lunch.

The two women ate their meal in tense silence, ears tuned for the sound of the front door opening signalling the men's' return. Finishing their meal they had washed up, Julie's mother by this time was in an even more pent up state, 'this is all you get, after being married all these years, I wanted it to be a nice meal with us all sitting down together, and what happens,' she picked up the dishcloth angrily. At that moment the front door opened and the two men walked in. Entering the kitchen Phil Spencer asked 'is dinner ready?' Eva turned around angrily, she could not contain herself and in an angry gesture she flung the dishcloth at her husband. 'Now then mother, there's no need to be like that.' Phil Spencer picked up the dishcloth and placed it back on the sink. 'You just sit down and me and Colin'll help ourselves to some dinner.'

Just as it Was

'Dinner, dinner, it's nearly tea-time and your dinners all dried up.'

'We don't mind, we don't mind at all, it's been nice we've been in some good company haven't we Colin. Sorry we're late.'

'Come on Colin sit down the dinner's just about acceptable after all this time,' Julie pulled out a chair for him, 'it's not Mum's fault though.' Colin looked as though he was about to make a dash for it, he had upset Julie and Mrs Spencer's temper had put the fear of God in him. Would he be next to receive her rebukes. He sat down nervously and began to eat. 'It's very nice Mrs Spencer,' he was trying to soothe things over a bit. Mrs Spencer had already got her coat on, 'I'm taking the dog for a walk, I hope that when I get back the pots will be washed.'

After the men had eaten Julie's dad said that he was going for a lie down. Julie had tidied everything up in the kitchen with Colin trailing behind her trying to help. 'Your Dad really didn't realise how late he was you know.'

'You were there Colin, you could have done something about it.'

'But he met some friends, nice people, and he tells a very good tale.'

'Oh I know that alright, I also know how much trouble Mum had gone to with the dinner.'

'Does she often get upset like that, she was in a real temper, I've never seen her like that before.'

Just as it Was

'Well it doesn't happen as much as it used to, when we were small we never knew when a row might break out. She had a lot to put up with. She had a very hard life herself as a child, she was only twelve when her mother died and she was the only girl in a houseful of brothers. Her father had died a few years earlier and when war broke out four of her brothers enlisted and two of them were killed and two died shortly after the war from injuries they'd received. After the war she married Dad but things got hard, Dad walked to Yorkshire to find a job on the railway. I think that Mum was in such a state that running her home to a timetable was the only security that she had and she's kept it up ever since. Things have been better between her and Dad since we got a bit older although when he goes out to the pub we still dread it if he comes back late. I did think it would be O.K. today Colin because you were with him, but I was wrong wasn't I?'

'Don't blame me Julie, I couldn't do anything about it.'

'Well I'm sorry that it happened when you were here, it's the pub that causes the trouble, they get on most of the time now.'

'What about us Julie, how are we getting on, you haven't been writing to me very often recently?'

'I don't have much time for writing, in fact I don't seem to have much time for anything apart from work and studying.'

'Well I'm the same, and I never seem to get to see much of you, even when I come home.'

'Perhaps you'd be better off if we finished, you could do what you wanted in Richmond then.'

Just as it Was

'Is that what you want, do you still love me Julie.'

'Colin at the moment I don't know what I feel, I'm very upset about what's happened here today I'm tired, and I've too much to do, I certainly don't want the sort of life that my Mum and Dad have had.'

'Well come to Canada with me, we can start a whole new life together out there.'

'Canada! I'm right in the middle of my training how can I think about anything else at the moment?'

'Well whatever you're thinking about I don't think it's me I better go home, I'll see you sometime Julie, bye.'

Just as it Was

13

Moving On

As she moved about getting ready to go on duty again Julie reflected on what had happened between her and Colin the day before. Perhaps a spell apart wont do any harm, give us a chance to meet other people of the opposite sex, she told herself. They were both very young when they met and this up until now, was the only enduring relationship for both of them and apart from that the fact that they were so far apart geographically didn't help. I'm going to forget about Colin for a while and concentrate on getting my State Registration she told herself. In spite of this she looked for a letter from him for a week or two, after all it was him who had walked out. There was nothing in the post and she resigned herself to the fact that their going out together had come to an end.

Her spell on night duty was also shortly to end and she found herself moved onto the adjoining female orthopaedic ward on day duty. Her duties now were more responsible and after successfully passing her Preliminary Nursing examination she got her checks and was more heavily involved in nursing processes. She worked her way through giving enemas, taking pulse and temperatures and assuming the duties of the ward nurse in theatre. There was a possessive nature about

Just as it Was

the status of their seniority among the nurses which served them well as they revelled in their ability to take on more tasks. The patients were long stay some of them in plaster casts due to spinal injuries and even the cartilage operations were in for ten days or so, the opportunity to get to know the patients made the work more interesting. Doreen Stapleton had been on the ward for several weeks when Julie moved there and a close friendship built up between the two. Doreen was in her mid forties and she had a deformity of the spine which after recent surgery had resulted in her being in a full plaster cast in which she had to be turned regularly to avoid pressure sores. Doreen was a single lady and in spite of her handicap which she had been born with she had enjoyed a full life before her condition deteriorated. Coming from a well established professional family she told her enthralled audience of the theatres that she had visited. As the nurses attended to her at length she told them stories of the wonderful hotels where she had gone out to dinner and enjoyed Dover Sole or Fillet steaks helped down by fine wines followed by Pavlovas and Tarte-Tatin served with the desert wine 'La Flora Blanche' her particular favourite. She spoke of potted palms, music from grand piano and violin as waistcoated waiters with napkins neatly folded over their forearm waited on them. Most of the girls had never experienced such a thing but they didn't envy Doreen the memories of happier times and some of them even dreamt that one day they might also enjoy them. Doreen told the stories in a nostalgic way, something which belonged to her distant past something which she had enjoyed and perhaps this was a sort of

Just as it Was

compensation for the trauma that she was going through now. There were still weeks of treatment ahead of her and the treatment was palliative rather than a cure. 'We're having a Christmas ball in the hospital in a few weeks time,' Julie was taking the patient's temperatures and she had stopped by Doreen Stapleton's bed.

'Are you going?'

'Yes I think so, I've never been to a ball before.'

'What are you going to wear?'

'I'll have to buy something, I need a long dress so I'm told.'

'Will you do something for me?'

'What is it Doreen?'

'I've got a lovely necklace, it isn't of great value but it is a lovely piece and it deserves an outing, I want you to wear it.'

'Oh that's so kind of you but I don't think that I ought, I don't know what matron would say.'

'Well I don't want you to get into trouble and I'm only lending it to you, these things are just lying around uselessly and it really would give me a lot of pleasure if you wore my necklace at the ball.' Julie was very touched by the woman's generosity, but worried about what some others might think. 'I'd be pleased to wear it;' she said although she thought to herself I hope that she forgets all about it now as she moved along to the next patient. Borrowing from patients even when it was suggested by them was something that Julie was uncomfortable with.

Just as it Was

John Gibson had been delighted when he saw that Nurse Spencer was now part of the day staff on the female orthopaedic ward. She had caught his eye that very first day in outpatients when she asked him to sign the drugs request and he had never forgotten her. Today he had accompanied the consultant on the ward round and now together with sister he and Mr Warner were discussing the next week's admissions. Staff nurse came from Sister's office into the kitchen with the silver percolator and the white china cups on a tray to make the coffee for them all as they discussed the order of the operating list. Julie was hurriedly grabbing a drink in the kitchen before she began testing the urines. 'Nurse Spencer will you set up a tray and dress Mrs Johnson's leg Mr Warner disturbed it on his round, just a gauze dressing that's all that's needed.'

'Yes staff, I was just about to test the urines but I'll do the dressing first.'

'Thank you' Staff nurse took the coffee tray back into the office where the others had almost finished discussing the 'list'. The sound of Dr Gibson's pager disturbed the conversation, he took the gadget out of the top pocket of his white coat. 'Oh I promised to look at a patient on ward four, they're asking me if I can go in the next half -hour.'

'I think our business here is finished,' Mr Warner leaned back expansively in his chair 'you go and see what you can do for them on ward four. I have a clinic in out-patients shortly.' The young doctor made his way out of the office towards the ward door. As he walked past the sterilizer room he caught sight of Nurse Spencer setting up a dressing tray. She had her back

Just as it Was

towards him but he recognised the slim waist and the way she wore her neat nurses hat pinned over her tumbling chestnut hair. He called to her. 'Hello Nurse Spencer, I wondered when we would meet again.' She turned around at the sound of his voice and blushed as she looked at him, not knowing what to say.'

'I saw you on the tennis court last week, do you play much?'

'Not really, Nurse Wialker asked me to have a game before winter really sets in. I used to enjoy playing when I was at school, and sometimes at the week-end in the local park, I don't get much chance to play now.'

He looked at her and smiled encouragingly. 'I'm trying to arrange a doubles, would you have a game with me?'

What! silently Julie's heart gave a leap, the heart throb of the hospital was asking her to play tennis with him. 'I don't think I'm good enough for that.'

'You looked pretty good to me,'

'No I'm not, I'm really not very good.'

'Well I'm not a professional, neither are the other pair, you'll be fine.'

Julie thought about it, a game of tennis with John Gibson would break the monotony of her private life at the moment and she was coming around to the idea.'

'When do you want to play?'

'Can you make it tomorrow afternoon?'

'I've a two to four, is that long enough.'

Just as it Was

John Gibson smiled. 'That's perfect, see you on the tennis court at half-past two.'

The other's had already assembled as Julie walked onto the court wearing a cotton skirt and top and a pair of plimsolls. She was a bit unnerved to see that the pair whom she and John Gibson were playing was the R.S.O. and one of her colleagues, a nurse who was a year senior to her and who was kitted out in tennis club style. John greeted her and the other two joined them. 'What are we going to do, the best of three sets?' Paul Graham the resident surgical officer waited for John to reply. 'That sounds fine to me shall we have a bit of a knock about first, just to warm up?'

We've got a nice afternoon anyway.' Julie looked at the other girl, she had worked with her and found her to be quite pleasant. She was one of a group whose family came from a very wealthy residential area of Leeds and her experience and background were very different from Julie's home life. Julie's opinion of her was that she was a bit scatty and spoilt and they really didn't have much in common. I'll have to try hard to keep up with this lot I bet that they play tennis every week. The truth was that Julie was not particularly sporty, she played hockey and tennis at school and swam and climbed the ropes and jumped the horses in the gym but all moderately. She was not an athlete she could swim a bit, and run a bit but that was all. Why oh why had she agreed to play tennis today? They took up their positions and John was first to serve. He accurately hit the ball in and Paul Graham struggled to reach it and whack it back into Julie's area, it fell to her left

Just as it Was

and with a scoop of her racket she back-handed it over the net to the edge of the tramlines on the opponents side where Brenda failed to reach it. 'Shot Julie.' John's enthusiasm echoed through the air and Julie felt her self confidence rise. The game went to one set all and in the final set the sky darkened and play was stopped. 'Let's have a cup of tea in the nurses home.' Brenda and the R.S.O. led the way followed by the other two. 'Phew that was good' John sat down in one of the comfy armchairs as Brenda went off to the kitchen to make the tea. 'I'll help her with the tray' Paul said and made his way out of the room.

'You played very well Nurse Spencer' John smiled at Julie, 'we must play again.'

'We'll be lucky to play again this year, the season should be over already.'

'Perhaps we could do something else, what do you like to do?'

'Sometimes I go dancing, and I like to watch a film.'

John looked a bit doubtful, 'I'm not much of a dancer, perhaps you could teach me.'

'I'm going to the Fairgrove on Saturday, if you want to come along perhaps I can help you to learn to dance.'

'I would very much like that Julie but I can't manage Saturday, perhaps we could do something in the week.'

'Actually there's a dance in the Badminton Hall tonight, one of the monthly bashes they're good fun and I thought that I might pop in after duty just for an hour or so.'

Just as it Was

'I think that I could manage that,' John smiled at her broadly, 'see you there about nine o'clock then.'

She had packed a dress, some make up and a pair of shoes into a bag before leaving home that morning and Julie was now freshening her appearance in the cloakroom. As she combed through her hair and slipped the full skirted dress over her head Vera looked on enviously.

'How do you do it Julie, five minutes and you turn yourself into a glamour girl, I'd have to have a couple of hours in a hairdressers and a beauty parlour to get that look, are you in love or something.'

'Just excited I love dancing Vera, she turned to her friend, 'why aren't you coming to the dance?'

'Dennis is meeting me, he doesn't like dancing all that much.'

'Oh well just make sure that he's got plenty of petrol in his car, you don't want to get stuck down a country lane again.'

'Hey you less of that, we're getting married next year after I've taken my finals, can't wait.'

'Don't talk about finals, I should be writing up my lecture on the circulatory system tonight, I'll have to stay in for the rest of the week.' Vera buckled up her gabardine and pinned her veil to her hair, 'have a good time, and don't miss the last bus to Wysten,' she called as she walked out.

The music was playing loudly as Julie got to the dance, there was no sign of John and she joined a group of other second

Just as it Was

year nurses and as was the way with them they were discussing the experiences of the day. One of them a girl who lived in and whom Julie knew very little of was describing how she had been sent down to theatre with a patient and how Mr Sinclair the anaesthetist had shown her how to hold the man's chin up to extend the trachea after intubating him and so give a clear passage in the airways. She joined in their conversation making a note of the fact that even after coming off duty the day's work was still with them and how hard it was to shake off the fact that they were all nurses in training. 'Look who's just come in,' Joan from outpatients spoke to the others. 'It's John Gibson I haven't seen him here before, crikey he's coming over to us,' she put on a smile and hoped that he would ask her to dance, after all she had been working with him earlier in casualty and he had been quite chatty. 'Are you girls enjoying yourselves?' John addressed himself to the group and there were smiles all round, 'I'm spoilt for choice' he said, 'how about you Nurse Spencer, would you like to waltz?' Julie said that she would and they took to the dance floor leaving the others asking themselves why he hadn't chosen them. 'You're looking very nice tonight Nurse Spencer' John looked at Julie appreciatively.

'Nice of you to say so but I'm feeling rather hot it's a bit crowded in here, also I have to tell you that I can't stay long I have to catch the bus home. If I'm to teach you to dance we better get a move on.'

'I've got a better idea, a couple of dances and then we'll take a breather there are too many people in here.'

Just as it Was

Julie shivered as they walked into the hospital grounds, 'here' John took off his jacket and put it around her shoulders. The warmth of the afternoon was gone, replaced by a cool gusty evening breeze.'What about you, you'll get a chill you're in your shirtsleeves now?'

'Don't worry about me, I'm fine, come on let's go and sit on the bench by the tennis court.' 'The night was pitch black as they gingerly felt their way around to the seat. The moon had disappeared but suddenly the clouds shifted and the court where they had played that afternoon was highlighted. The wire grid around the play area stood firmly in the shadows and was illuminated briefly as the clouds quickly drifted across the sky and then plunged them into darkness again. Julie closed her eyes thinking of the game of tennis that they had played only a few hours ago and she felt confident after the good performance that she had managed to put in. John had been lavish in his praise and she looked forward to perhaps, playing with him again. Faint music sounded from the hall from where they had just escaped, it had been so stiflingly warm in there and now it was refreshing to be out in the open. As they sat side by side, John glanced at Julie's profile. She was looking forward an inscrutable look on her face. Her smoothly carved cheekbones and her brow onto which her hair tumbled and was ruffled by the wind melted his being. This girl had an effect on him from the very moment that he saw her. Her youth and her innocence made him want to protect her from the world. 'How can you stand being a nurse?' he took her hand.

'What do you mean it's what I've chosen to do?'

Just as it Was

'But some of the things that you have to do are so distasteful so downright unsuitable for you, it's so unpleasant at times nursing.'

'Dr Gibson' (reverting to his occupational title.) I don't find them distasteful, in fact half the time I don't think about what I'm actually doing, I just think of it as helping people.' He turned her around to face him and he leaned towards her. Her hair brushed his face and he gently touched her brow smoothing her hair back and pulling her body closer to his kissing her tenderly. 'I think that you're much too young and pretty to be doing these things nursing can be quite crude and the name is John.'

'John, you really don't know much about me; I haven't been wrapped up in cotton wool you know. I come from a working class background and I live in a terrace house with the rest of my family. I have often come across the less attractive side of life and of human beings and I can cope. There are plenty of others just like me who come into nursing, it's a vocation, we all want to be Florence Nightingale.'

'You should be sheltered from the unsavoury things in life a young girl like you.'

'John I'm tough, perhaps you were brought up differently but my family have struggled against unemployment, poverty, six of us crowded into a small house living in one room most of the time. I'm not a delicate flower I know what life's all about.'

Just as it Was

'Julie, I still think that you should be protected, but I didn't know anything about you, you seem so innocent and vulnerable.'

'Well you know now, I think that you probably come from a very different background to me.'

'Does it matter?'

'Yes John, I think that it does, in fact I'm very sure that it does I look at life differently.'

'It doesn't matter to me.' He took her in his arms and kissed her again this time with a passionate urgency to her surprise she found herself responding, the attraction was irresistible. Slowly she drew away from him, 'I'm sorry John, perhaps we shouldn't see each other again this just doesn't seem right, please let me go.'

'I'm sorry, if I've upset you I apologise, I'd like us to go on seeing each other. Please, let me take you out on your next day off, no strings we could go the cinema, or something, let's remain friends at least.' Surely it couldn't hurt to meet him again he was very attractive and what could be more harmless than a visit to the cinema she needed a friend at the moment. Colin was in the past and to have a friend, a boyfriend to go out with would surely make life more interesting and exciting. 'I'd like that, I'd like to go to the cinema with you I'll have a look at next week's off duty and we can sort something out.' After all he had said no strings.

Just as it Was

14

The Hospital Ball

Julie had a day off and she was walking with her sister along the long frost covered lane which led to the 'Clear Springs.' It was a favourite walk one which the family had often taken together in summertime. When the children were young they had loved to jump from one side of the banking to the other and if it was very warm they took off their shoes and paddled. Today there was just the two of them she and Babs were exercising the dog and taking in a bit of fresh air. Well wrapped up in winter coats and boots after being cooped up in the stuffy living room at home they were enjoying the winter scenery and chatting. 'We're having a ball at the hospital.'

'Are you going?'

'I'd love to but I'm not sure, I wouldn't know what to wear, I've never been to a ball before.'

'Well neither have I, but but Dr Ryan's wife used to wear beautiful long dresses when they went to formal balls.'

'I'll have to buy one then' she hesitated 'that's if I decide to go.'

'I'll come with you if you like, to buy a dress I mean.'

'Would you, oh thanks Babs I've no idea what to buy.'

Just as it Was

'Perhaps we could have a trip out we could go to Sheffield on your next off duty there should be something there to suit you.'

'What about clothing coupons?'

Clothing coupons shouldn't be a problem they're a bit more relaxed about them now.'

'I've still got most of mine anyway, I'm in uniform most of the time, I haven't bought anything new for ages.'

'That's fine then, we'll go next week.'

On Julie's day off the two walked up the street and caught the Sheffield bus at the stop on the main road. They settled back to enjoy the ride into the city. The bus took them through Consiborough with it's Castle perched high on a hill overlooking the small town and as the road stretched out over open countryside they were given lovely views over the Dearne valley. The girls talked little as they took in the scenery enjoying the treat of getting away from industrialisation for a a little while. Travelling on through Rotherham the landscape took on an industrial look again and it increased as they travelled past the steelworks with their belching chimneys. Rows of houses and small shops closely lined the road into the city, grocery stores, greengrocers, post offices and many more small family businesses. The pavements were full of shoppers, people stopped to talk to each other and the familiar urban scene brought Julie and Babs back to reality. Very shortly they reached Sheffied and the passengers spilled out onto the pavement at the bus

Just as it Was

station. Babs and Julie made their way up onto the Moor. There was still evidence of the destruction caused in December nineteen forty when there had been a heavy blitz on the city by German bombers and although a speedy restoration of the devastation had been made there were still occasional piles of rubble and some damaged buildings to be seen. The Moor had been ablaze as the planes had dropped incendiary bombs. Julie remembered how they had trembled in their Anderson shelter in Doncaster as they listened to the planes going over to and from their destination and how they had agonised over the terrible onslaught meted out to the citizens of Sheffield. Now the city was open for business and along the busy streets they made their way to Coles a quality and long established store where they chose to look for the dress. Julie was excited at the prospect of shopping for a ball gown but as she searched along the rails the choice was limited and after trying on one or two, which she thought, might be suitable she wasn't happy about any them. 'Can I help?' an assistant approached them.

'I'm looking for something special for a dance that I'm going to, well actually it's going to be a bit grand, it's a ball.'

'I think I have just the thing for you.' The assistant disappeared for a few minutes then came back carrying an armful of multi layered white net dress. It was off the shoulders with an adornment of gold spots on the bodice and edged by a neat frill. Julie looked at it warily.

'A bit daring isn't it?'

Just as it Was

'Try it on, I'm sure that you'll look lovely in it.' Julie followed the woman into the changing room and looked at herself through the long mirror. She wasn't too sure about the expanse of flesh that she was showing. 'There you can carry it off,' the assistant had helped Julie into the dress, 'you've got the figure and the looks.'

'I don't know, I've never worn anything like this before, what do you think Babs?'

'Perhaps you could have a little net stole to put around your shoulders, you do look nice in it.' Her sister smiled encouragingly.

'How much is it going to cost with a stole?'

'I could let you have both for five guineas' the assistant smiled.

'That's nearly a month's wages.'

'Well I can see what the manageress says to five pounds if you like.' she was keen to make a sale. Julie nodded her head, 'It is a special occasion.'

With a smile on her face and the message that the manageress had agreed to the price the assistant was soon back. Julie looked at the dress and swallowed hard as she thought of the few pounds that she had saved in her post office savings book. After pondering she quickly said 'I'll take it.'

'You'll be the belle of the ball.'

Crikey thought Julie, more like Cinderella when I look at my bank book.

Just as it Was

As the date for the ball drew nearer it was the main topic of conversation between those who were able to go. 'Who are you bringing?' the question was being tossed around the table as the first dinner nurses ate their meal. 'Are you bringing Colin?'

Julie turned to Vera who had not been told of the split.'He's not on leave, I wont be bringing anybody.'

'Nurse Hartley smirked it had not gone unnoticed that Julie and Dr Gibson had been seen together on the tennis courts and chatting together in various parts of the hospital and his long spells when doing his nightly visit to the orthopaedic ward where Julie had worked and where he was houseman had also attracted a good deal of attention. 'I wonder if Dr Gibson'll be there, perhaps he'll dance with you.' Julie hadn't seen John for some weeks and as far as she was concerned it was just a friendly relationship and that was fine with her. 'I don't know what you mean, why should he?' she turned to her friend Vera 'are you bringing Dennis?'

'Of course,' Vera said.

Who are you bringing and what are you going to wear? the excitement grew and the conversation was of very little else between the excited young women. This was the first 'Ball' to be held at the hospital for a number of years and as many staff as possible were expected to be there. On the day itself Julie packed her dress, jewellery and shoes along with her make up into an overnight bag. She travelled to the hospital on the trolley bus and arriving there she made her way to the

Just as it Was

nurses home where Chris Walker had invited her to go and change in her room and together they would make their way across to the large outpatients area where the ball was to take place. 'Ready?' Chris called to her friend who after changing had come in from the bathroom.

'I feel a bit like a Christmas Tree.' It was true that with the dress and the diamante necklace earrings and bracelet all loaned by Doreen Stapleton, Julie presented a sparkling picture.

Chris laughed, 'don't get cold feet now, you've paid a fortune for the dress, let's go and show it off.'

Sister Robinson and her army of helpers had transformed the outpatient's hall decorating it with ribbons and floral arrangements and setting out tables and chairs on the edge of the maple wood floor, which had been polished to a fine finish for the dancing. A small orchestra was set up at one end of the room and a bar had been opened with soft drinks and alcohol and groups of people were sitting at the tables laughing and chatting to one another. There were couples already dancing and Julie was pleased to see that there were others apart from herself in elaborate dresses. Some of the men were dressed formally in dinner jackets while others wore smart lounge suits, She felt more at ease as she looked around and as a young man whom she had previously danced with in the relaxed atmosphere of the Badminton Hall asked her to take to the floor for a quick step she gladly accepted.

Just as it Was

'Come and join us at our table.' As the dance finished Peter the young man invited Julie to join him and another couple at one of the tables, which were quickly being taken up. 'What about my friend Christine I came with her?'

'Bring her over, the more the merrier.' Julie found her friend and invited her to join the group. 'What will you have to drink?'

'An orange juice for me please.'

'And me' said Chris as the young man looked at her inquisitively. Peter and his friend Michael went off to the bar to fetch drinks for the group as the girls introduced themselves to each other. 'Michael and I met in the physio department' Pat said. 'I've worked there for six months now and he's been there for about two years. We invited Peter to come because he has a thing about nurses, he's been out with one or two, he's an old friend of ours.'

'My boy friend's in the army, he couldn't get away for the dance' Julie thought that she better declare her status before she got coupled up with Peter. Although she hadn't been in touch with Colin at all since the break up she still considered that one day they might get back together and she didn't like the look of Peter anyway.

'I'm free' Christine laughed as the men came back carrying the drinks.

Julie looked around the room, which was now filling up quite quickly. There were groups of girls standing together a bit self consciously obviously unused to the rather formal occasion. They chattered animatedly and cast their eyes about furtively

Just as it Was

hoping for the advance of dance partners. The more sophisticated ones were mingling with the dinner-jacketed set and she was pleased that she and Chris had been invited to join the others at the table. I do feel a bit out of my depth, she thought. It was certainly different from the dances in the Church hall which she had enjoyed with Babs and Doris and she wondered if she were the first one of her family to go to such an event. However the present company was not too taxing and in her posh gown, she felt eminently dressed for the occasion sparkling as she did. 'Look who's just come in.' Pat was looking around the room she was the sort of person who liked to keep abreast of things. On the other side of the big hall a well-dressed couple were being introduced to others at one of the tables. 'They're John Gibson's parents.'

'Do you know them, have you met them before then?'

'Occasionally when we've been out for meals, and sometimes at the tennis club, his father's a very successful banker and he's tipped to become group chief executive, and his mother's a stalwart of the hospital comforts fund very top drawer and really nice people.'

Chris kicked Julie's ankle under the table.

'How super' she said. Peter looked bored with the conversation.

'Come on Christine, would you like to dance?' he had taken the hint about Julie's boyfriend and switched his attention to the other nurse. They walked onto the floor and Julie was left alone with Pat and Michael. Feeling a bit like a gooseberry she excused saying 'I'll just go and powder my nose.' and she

Just as it Was

walked over to the cloakroom. As she was checking her hair in the mirror Vera walked in. 'Hello have you been here long?'

'Perhaps half an hour?'

'Are you on your own?'

'Not really, I came with Christine, she's dancing.'

'What about you have you been dancing?'

'Yes I have.'

'Who with?'

'With Peter a boy that I've met before at the dances in the Badminton Hall.'

Vera was carefully applying more lipstick to her already ruby red lips. 'Well I don't think that you'll be dancing with Dr Gibson tonight, he's with a stunning looking girl, I saw them together as I came in.'

'You've been listening to too much gossip what makes you think I'm interested in him?'

'It's not just me, people have been talking but suit yourself, come on let's go into the dance.'

The girls joined Dennis, 'you're looking very glamorous tonight Julie' the young man looked at her appreciatively.

'Nice of you to say so Dennis.'

'It's a lovely dress,' Vera joined in the conversation, Julie felt a tap on her shoulder as the orchestra struck up a waltz. 'May I have this dance?' John Gibson was there smiling at her. Handsome and smart in his dinner jacket and bow tie he waited for an answer, she was taken off guard and not a little

Just as it Was

embarrassed but as she caught an unfathomable look in Vera's eye she nodded her head and smiled at John as they went onto the dance floor together. 'Are you enjoying yourself?'

'Yes thank you, it's wonderful it doesn't feel a bit like a hospital.'

'No they've transformed it, the floor feels pretty good for dancing.'

'Shame that some people are still working.'

'Yes we're the lucky ones,' just for an instant a picture of the night staff came into Julie's mind but she dismissed it instantly and decided then and there to enjoy herself. John Gibson wasn't the good dancer that Colin was but she enjoyed the waltz to the tune of 'Down In The Glen' and as he held her she felt comfortable and more than a little flattered. This handsome young doctor with whom a large number of the nursing staff were smitten had chosen her to dance with. Where was the stunning girl whom Vera had seen him with though? The dance ended and as they walked off the floor together John Gibson asked Julie if she would like a drink.

'Thank you that would be nice.'

'Let's find a table first, oh here's one just for two, a nice little table, now what can I get you, something to warm you up there's still a chill in the air there aren't enough people here yet to lift the temperature.' Julie had never drunk alcohol but tonight she wanted to appear sophisticated, what should she ask for. Her parents drank beer and shandies with just a bottle of sherry and one of port at Christmas. She

Just as it Was

remembered a conversation that she had with Aunty Freda on her last visit about a warming drink. 'I'll have a port and brandy please.' Little did she know that this would make a huge hole in John's houseman's salary but although inwardly shocked he handled it well and as he made his way to the bar he felt in his pocket to check that his funds were sufficient. The bar was busy and as John waited to be served he looked back across the room to where Julie was sitting at the table that he had just left. His heart lurched at the sight of her, he couldn't get her out of his mind and he was delighted that she had turned up on her own tonight. Their paths hadn't crossed recently and it seemed an age since they last went out together. 'Here we are' Dr Gibson put the drinks down on the table and sat facing Julie. 'I haven't seen you for ages, I kept expecting to see you on the ward but I never got a chance to speak to you when you were there. We did say that we would go to a dance together.'

Julie picked up her glass and took a sip of the potent spirit. It burnt her throat and she struggled to swallow it without making a fuss. 'Are you o.k?' John Gibson looked at her anxiously. What was it about this girl that attracted him so much, she was so young and looked so vulnerable. Very pretty! but there were lots of other pretty girls about. Her fragile delicacy and her tendency to blush modestly sat uneasily with the fact that she had chosen such a strong alcoholic drink. 'Is the drink alright?'

'It's perfect' she said feeling the effects of it curling her toes.

'Is it what you usually drink?'

Just as it Was

What should she say, was she going to have to let him know that she usually drank orange juice her attempt at sophistication would be shattered. She picked up the glass and took another sip. 'It's a lovely drink' she said evading his question, 'very warming' and as she took another sip. she felt a warmth and a feeling of relaxation sweep over her. 'Do you know, I feel like dancing, this is one of my favourite tunes.' The band had just struck up the very popular 'Orange Coloured Sky' and as they took to the dance floor, which was now pretty, crowded John greeted the girl he had been seen coming in with and whom Pat had pointed out. 'Someone you know?'

'Just a family friend, no one special.' Julie was feeling more and more lively, she was enjoying herself and when the dance finished and another quickstep was played they danced around the floor again. 'Phew, that was fun,' she picked up her glass on returning to the table and as John told her about his family she listened interestedly, sipping away at her drink and letting him do all the talking Julie was really enjoying herself. All around them people were laughing and chatting and as her friends walked past the table they said 'hello.' She was carried away as he told her about his childhood, how he and his brother had slid down banisters and built trolleys and had lots of fun together. She was just happy to listen and feel the enveloping warmth of her drink isolating her from others. The edges of reality were blurred and Julie was completely happy. When John paused and asked her to have another drink he was relieved to hear her ask for an orange juice. The evening passed in a whirl. John looked at his watch, 'oh

Just as it Was

crikey, no! I've got to leave you if you'll excuse me I've one or two duty dances to fulfil, I can't really get out of it without a fuss but I hate leaving you.'

'Don't worry I can join my friends at their table; it's been lovely John very pleasant I've enjoyed your company.'

But I'm coming back, I want the last waltz with you' John looked at her intently.

'Let's see how it goes, I'll go and join the others.' She was disappointed and then she shook herself, was he making excuses. Did he really intend to come back for the last waltz. Pat Michael and Peter greeted her with knowing smiles 'you've been gone a long time.'

'Well I'm back now, where's Christine.'

'She's just gone to have a word with someone she knows, come on then, let's dance Julie.' Peter took her elbow and led her onto the dance floor. As they got back to the others Christine was back sitting with them 'have you enjoyed yourself?' she asked.

'Yes Peter's a good dancer.'

'I don't mean Peter, I mean you and John Gibson.' The manner was high-spirited and Pat who had had rather too much to drink said 'Has he left you, gone back to his family and friends?' Julie felt hot and uncomfortable what had she been thinking of, perhaps Pat was right why had she spent most of the evening with him, they had nothing in common that was obvious from what he had told her about his family. Pat was right about his 'roots' and Julie knew that they were a million miles away from hers. But here he was walking

Just as it Was

towards her, well what will Pat have to say now? she thought and as he asked her again to dance, Julie took to the floor with him.

'Did you miss me?'

'Well I've certainly enjoyed myself it's been lovely. It's getting late now and I think that I'm going to have to leave soon,' Julie saw Christine approaching she was ready to go back to the nurses home. 'I'm sleeping here tonight and I don't want to get locked out.'

'Can I walk you across?' John looked at her holding on to her hand. In a rush of warmth and carried by the exuberance of the evening she said that he could and after gathering her coat and making her excuses to Chris they walked out together into the cold night air. There were a few people making their way across the pathway to the home but they thinned out as John and Julie got nearer to the porch. 'I really have enjoyed tonight, thank you.' Julie's head was still reeling from the excitement of the night and the after effect from the drink that she had earlier. I really shouldn't have had that she thought, and she struggled to get herself together.

'Julie I can't tell you how much fun it's been I must see you again please don't let's leave it so long 'til next time.' John moved towards her, took her arm and kissed her lightly on the cheek. 'John I must go in they'll be locking me out soon. I'd like to see you again, it has been fun, I don't know when though, I'll have to look at the off duty.'

'Well let me know, we'll fix up a drink and a dance. I really have enjoyed being with you tonight.'

Just as it Was

'I've enjoyed it too, thanks John, thank you for a lovely evening.' Julie walked into the nurses' home and John walked away along the path and back to the hospital.

Just as it Was

15

Getting Told Off

Julie was walking back to the ward after lunch in the nurses' dining room, as she turned to go through the door to the covered walkway she saw Dr Gibson walking towards her stethoscope hanging from his neck a boyish smile on his face, he stopped as he reached her. 'I'm glad that I've seen you, there's a dance at the tennis club a week on Saturday and I wondered if you would like to come with me if you could get the evening off.'

'That's a lot of ifs, I'm not sure, I don't know anyone at the tennis club.'

'I know lots of people they're a good crowd, Pat and Michael will be there you were with them at the hospital dance.'

'Well if you think so but I have to see if I can get the evening off first and my Dad will insist that I get the last bus home.'

'See what you can do, and let me know, I'll catch you on the ward, I'm in theatre this afternoon, I've just been writing up the pre-meds for tomorrows list.'

'I better get back the ward's busy at the moment, I don't think there's a spare bed anywhere, what about Miss Stapleton, do you think she'll be ready for home soon?'

Just as it Was

'Another week or so I think, then she's going to need lots of physio.'

'I shall miss her, she's been in a long time, she 's a big favourite with everybody, part of the furnishings.'

'It's funny how fond you can get of people when they've been in for a long time then you never see them again, apart from a check up in out-patients.'

'We're getting a bit philosophical here, it's the nature of the job.'

'I'll have to dash, let me know about the dance,' he took her hand and squeezed it.

Julie was surprised at the excitement that she felt, she was flattered by the attention and John Gibson was a very attractive young man but she really wasn't sure about the dance. The afternoon passed quickly patients who were for theatre were dressed in their op gowns painted with the antiseptic chlorhexadine over the surgical site and after making sure that dentures were removed the pre medication was given as their hour of surgery approached. There was a very special patient on the list today. The consultant orthopaedic surgeon's housekeeper was on the list for an operation to rid her of a bunion. 'I've put her in a corner of the ward with screens around her, Mr Warner wanted her to be as private as possible but I'm afraid that's the best that I can do' Sister said. 'Make sure that she's kept warm and comfortable behind there Staff, I'm off duty this evening so I'll leave her in the good hands of you and and nurse Spencer.' The patients were all returned safely to the ward after surgery

Just as it Was

and the nurses were kept busy attending to them and carrying out the usual ward routine. Just before going off duty Julie went behind the screens to Mrs Gregory. 'How are you feeling?'

'Not too bad nurse but I'm a bit chilly.'

'Oh dear, would you like me to get you another blanket?'

'Yes please, it's so cold tonight.' Julie went to the linen room but the shelves were almost empty where the blankets should have been. She searched high and low but all that she could find was a red woolly blanket which looked very cosy and new. 'I'll put this on her bed, this'll make her nice and warm she thought.' Staff Nurse Fields called to her. 'Come along Nurse Spencer, it's time that we were off duty, is Mrs Gregory O.K.?'

'She's fine now Staff. I've given her another blanket.'

'We'll let the night staff take over now then, come on let's go off duty it's been a very busy day.'

Miss McDermot had summoned Julie to Sister's office as she had done her morning round.

'Nurse Spencer, is it you who gave Mrs Gregory the red blanket last night,?'

'Yes Sister.'

'Well I have to tell you that Mr Warner visited her late last night at the same time as Night Sister was doing her round. There was a red blanket on the bed nurse.'

Just as it Was

'Yes sister I put it there, Mrs Gregory was cold and it's the only one that I could find.'

Miss McDermott glared at her.'Do you know what it means when a red blanket is put on a patient's bed nurse?, Night Sister was extremely alarmed and upset, particularly as Mr Warner was visiting, do you really not know what a red blanket is for nurse?'

'Not really Sister Mc Dermot but it was the only one there I thought that it might be for using on trolleys or something.' Miss Mc Dermot looked ready to explode, her eyes almost popped out of her head as she spat out the words. 'It's an isolation warning nurse, it means that it is only used in extreme circumstances when a patient is infectious. Night Sister had no idea why it had been put there and she had a lot of explaining to do to Mr Warner who was quite unaware until Sister arrived that anything was wrong.'

'I didn't know that, I just knew that the patient was cold and that being the only blanket it looked so warm and cosy I thought that it would keep her warm, I thought it would be fine.'

'It was not fine nurse, it has caused a great deal of consternation and you mustn't do anything like that again you have caused a great deal of upset.' and with that she turned around and walked out of the office with Julie fighting back the tears. She stood there for a minute or two and then anger whelmed up inside her, how was I to know that it was an isolation blanket, nobody ever mentioned red blankets to me, it's so unfair. The more that she thought about it the more

Just as it Was

upset she got. How could she have been expected to know, Mrs Gregory was cold and she Julie had done her best for her. Such a fuss about it, I've had enough, I'm fed up and for two pins I'd pack it all in. The injustice was too much for her to cope with.

'Nurse Spencer what you are you doing here?' Staff Nurse had come into the office to open the drug cupboard for the medicine round and she found Julie in quite a state with herself. She felt so unfairly dealt with, no-one had told her about red blankets and the assistant matron had just wiped the floor with her.

'I'm leaving, I've had enough, I do my best and I keep getting told off, I'm going home.'

'Sit down a minute, I've heard about the red blanket episode, don't let it upset you. It's a long time since Miss McDermot was on the wards and she's probably forgotten what it's like sometimes. You've done very well since you've been on this ward and you mustn't get so upset. We all get told off in the heat of the moment, sometimes it's deserved; and sometimes not but you can't leave just because of a red blanket. Now go back on the ward and try to forget about it.' Julie sniffed and then calmed down a little at the senior nurse's words. She knew herself well, on previous occasions she had acted hastily and later regretted the consequences, perhaps she should think again. 'I don't think it was fair that I was told off for something that I wasn't told about. I love nursing though and I don't really want to leave. She took a big breath 'thank you staff for calming me down and being so nice. I will try to

Just as it Was

forget about it, I'm not going to waste two years training for something I couldn't help, I'll go back on the ward now and apologise to Mrs Gregory.'

Just as it Was

16

The Tennis Club Dance

Chris Walker and Julie had gone into Hodgson and Hepworths for coffee in their morning off duty. The smell of the freshly ground coffee assailed them and whetted their appetite as they walked through the grocery department where wonderful hams from which the assistants were slicing the amount the customers required from the bone, were displayed behind the glass fronted cabinets. The mahogany shelving gave a look of quality and solidity to the store and the variety of freshly baked bread and cakes, mouth watering bottled fruits; whole yellow cling Californian peaches and the luxury boxed chocolates were a feast for the eyes. The shoppers were a mixed bunch well dressed wives of the professional and better off families who did the bulk of their shopping there while the less well off spent some of their money on a rare treat for their families. Julie remembered how during the war her mother had regularly waited until late Saturday afternoon when trade was almost finished to go in for a quarter of ham and ask for the ham bone which always had some meat left clinging to it. It helped out with the rationing. Going upstairs to the café the girls found a table and ordered coffee and cakes, a mixed plate which they quickly devoured. The place was almost full with groups of

Just as it Was

housewives who obviously met up regularly chatting animatedly to each other. In their uniforms the two girls stood out and occasionally people would speak to them. 'hello nurse' ex-patients no doubt but they were left alone to enjoy their break.

'John Gibson has asked me to go to a tennis club dance with him.'

'What did you say.'

'I said I'd let him know if I can get the evening off.'

'And what about Colin?'

'I still haven't heard from him, he's probably got another girl friend in Richmond.'

'Why don't you write to him?

'Why doesn't he write to me?'

'A bit of a stalemate then, do you like John Gibson?'

'Who wouldn't like him, he's dishy and he's very nice. I've never been out with anyone like him before.'

'Well it's up to you, do your family know that you're getting friendly with one of the doctors.'

I haven't said anything up to now, but I know what you mean, we're only friends anyway.'

'Careful what you're doing Julie, you could end up getting hurt. Come on anyway I want to look at the shops before I go back on duty.'

Just as it Was

Julie thought about what her friend had said and as she and her mother were in the house alone she broached the subject. 'Mum I've been invited to go to a dance with someone a week on Saturday.'

'Where is it and who's asked you to go.'

'It's at the tennis club and one of the doctors at the hospital has asked me to go with him his name's Dr Gibson.'

Mrs Spencer spun around from the sink, 'YOU WHAT!'

'He's very nice Mum.'

'Very nice, who do think you are, going out with doctors, I knew going to the girls high school wouldn't do you any good. Just remember where you come from.'

'But we're only friends Mum, it's only a dance and I am nearly nineteen now.'

'.Don't say anything to your dad and forget about this Dr Gibson, stick to your own sort, Colin was a nice lad, why didn't you keep with him, you've got too many big ideas.'

'I've told my family about going to the tennis club dance Chris, at least I've told my Mum.'

'What did she say?'

'She was angry, she told me that I was getting too big for my boots and not to mention it to Dad.'

'She didn't actually say that you couldn't go then.'

Just as it Was

'Well no I don't suppose that she did.' Julie knew full well that those were her mother's intentions but she had got the Saturday evening off duty and as she usually went dancing on her Saturday night off would it really matter to them where she went. I'm not a child any longer, and I intend to go to this dance with John Gibson, I like him and perhaps I might even enjoy it, she told herself. Although she was determined to accept Dr Gibson's invitation she was nevertheless anxious about the evening. Her dress was no problem Julie had always had an eye for smart quality clothing, and on her anything looked good anyway, she felt that in the dress department she could hold her own, but what about the conversation what did they talk about at the tennis club?'

'I'll pick you up.' John was delighted when Julie told him that she was able to join him at the dance.

'Oh no really, I'd rather you didn't I'll make my own way to the club, it's better that way.'

John didn't know what was better about it but he was pleased that she was coming and he decided not to push it.

'Don't you be late home, make sure that you're on the last bus. Phil Spencer looked at his youngest daughter with pride. In her wrap over style slim fitting skirt, and her pretty powder blue top 'she looks like a young lady' he told himself. Her hair was brushed to fall over her brow and was curled under at the back into a pageboy and she had just enough make up on to make herself look more attractive. Not like some of them he thought, painted up to the eyes. She kissed her parents saying 'bye, I wont be late home, I'll be sure I'm on that bus'

Just as it Was

and she went out of the house with more than a little feeling of guilt.

Julie arrived at the tennis club as the dance was in full swing. The hall was big enough to take about eighty people at a guess and there were several couples dancing to the tune of 'My Foolish Heart.' She took a deep breath and was sure that she could smell the fragrance of tennis shoes and sweaty t-shirts, but an effort had been made to turn the place into a suitable venue for tonight's enjoyment. 'Are you looking for somewhere to put your coat?' John was there at her side obviously he had been looking out for her. 'Just pop in there and I'll get us a drink, what would you like?' She smiled to herself as she asked for an orange juice, thinking of the time she had asked for a port and brandy. No need to pretend now she would just be herself and they would have to take her as they found her. 'I'll introduce you to some people,' John Gibson approached a mixed group of men and women who all smiled at her in a friendly fashion. This is John and Tom and Liz, there were others but she knew that she wouldn't remember their names. 'You work at the hospital' Liz said her voice was upper class perfectly pronounced public school and for a minute Julie felt out of place she looked at John and seeing him smile she answered confidently in her perfectly spoken Yorkshire accent. 'Yes,' she said 'I'm training to be a nurse, I'm well into my second year.' Pat and Michael were approaching; the couple whom she had met at the hospital ball. 'Hello Julie, what a nice surprise, I didn't expect to see you here,' Michael slipped his arm around her waist and gave

Just as it Was

her a peck on the cheek as the others moved away, 'you're looking stunning tonight.' Pat raised her eyebrows but even she was impressed at the girls appearance and composure 'what a surprise, I didn't expect to see you here, do you know any of the others?' Julie saw a couple approaching and in a surprised voice she said 'yes I do have friends here.'

'Julie how lovely to see you.' She turned to John and the others as she said , 'this is Mrs Stocks my ex music teacher;' the woman smiled fondly at Julie and said 'and you all know my husband I'm sure' as she turned to the jolly round faced man at her side. The other three smiled and said 'hello.'

'Have you joined the tennis club Julie?'

'Oh no I'm here with my friend, just here for the night out and the dancing'.

'Well enjoy it and come again it's lovely to see you, we know John, perhaps he'll bring you again, you should think about joining the club.' As the others moved away Michael and Pat took their leave and walked onto the dance floor. 'You didn't tell me that you knew David Stocks our club secretary.'

'I didn't know, I didn't know that he was anything to do with the tennis club, Mrs Stocks was my music teacher. I had lessons from her for years until I left school.'

'I didn't know that you studied music.'

'There's a lot that we don't know about each other you don't really know much about me at all John.'

'We've plenty of time to get to know each other I hope, come on let's dance, I want to dance with you, you mysterious girl.'

Just as it Was

John took her arm and they walked together onto the dance floor. He drew her closely to himself as the music played 'Can't help Falling In Love With You.' and he rested his chin on her head 'I don't know much about you either,' she was beginning to feel more relaxed, she felt comfortable with him and she was glad that she had come. The dance ended and the musical trio big bass player announced that there would be a break in the dancing for refreshments. 'Would you like something to eat?'

'I'm really not hungry' she said, thinking of the huge tea that her mother had prepared before she left home.

'I'll just take a sausage roll and a cup of tea, it's a bit warm in here, there's a verandah shall we go and sit outside?'

'Yes, that would be lovely, I'll get my coat it could be quite cool out there.' There was no one else on the verandah and they each took a chair, John quickly ate his snack and drank his tea. 'Well?'

'What do you mean well?'

'I mean are you enjoying yourself and thank you for coming.'

'I am enjoying myself.'

'Julie,' he leaned across the small table and took hold of both her hands. 'I'm in love with you'

'John that's crazy.'

'Well it can't be such a surprise. Really I am absolutely mad about you. I can't stop thinking about you.'

'Stop it, please stop this now.'

Just as it Was

'I can't, I dream about you and when I'm going about the hospital I'm always looking for you.' He bent his head for a moment and Julie felt herself almost, almost, but she couldn't let this go on. 'John,' she pulled her hands away gently. 'John we hardly know each other.'

'We can get to know each other, I've never felt like this before Julie, I want to know all about you.'

'I've told you before it wont work, my family are working class yours are top notch upper class.'

'My parents are very aware of how different people live Julie, there's nothing stuffy about them, I know that they'd love you. He got up and walked round the table pulling her onto her feet. She found herself in his arms and as he kissed her she found herself responding. He let her go, 'you do feel something for me, there is a chance for us.'

'I don't know John I think it's impossible, I do like you but I don't think that either of us could change from what we are, I don't think that there's a future for us together.'

'I would love to take you to meet my family.'

'My family wouldn't know how to behave if I took you home, Mum was horrified when I said that I was going to a dance with a doctor. You're from the upper classes and for her you might as well be on a different planet. The problem probably lies more with them than with your parents, but please try to understand I can't make them feel uncomfortable. They're loving, kind, hard-working. I'm not enjoying having to explain all this but they haven't had the advantages of education and

Just as it Was

all that it brings with it and living on top of one another causes friction and sometimes up goes the balloon. I love them John, my family are working class and comfortable with that, they can't and don't want to mix outside their own class and I don't want to make them unhappy. They're my family and I'm part of them.'

'But I don't want to be with them particularly, it's you that I want to be with. I can understand how you feel, it's not important.'

'It is they'd expect me to take my boyfriend home.'

'Well take me to meet them don't tell them what I do.'

'It's the first thing that they'll ask me.'

'Tell them I'm a travelling salesman.'

'Ooh Dad'll be delighted at that, we can only be friends John, come on let's get back to the dance, and let's not think about the future.'

Just as it Was

17

Going To London

Julie's time on the female orthopaedic ward had come to an end and she was moved onto children's medical. This meant that she saw very little of John unless their paths crossed on the corridors as they went about their visits to the dining room and other departments. This morning she had visited the dispensary and on her way out he was walking along the corridor towards her. They had agreed to see each other for visits to the cinema and had met up as he took her out for runs in his nippy little M.G. sports car. She enjoyed these outings and he had agreed that their friendship should continue in this way hoping that he would win her over as time went by. 'Hello, I'm glad I've seen you, I want to ask you something.'

'Hello Dr Gibson' she smiled teasingly, 'hope it wont take long I've got to get back to the ward.'

'There's a dance at the Danum, Dad's lot have put it on, dinner and dance actually and I need a partner, will you come with me?'

'Ooh, I've got a holiday coming up and I'm going to London next week, when is the dinner dance?'

Just as it Was

'It's the beginning of next month, you'll be back by then.'

'How soon do you need to know, can I leave it until I come back from holiday?'

'Of course you can, I want you to meet my parents.'

'O.K. I'll have to sort out my off duty so leave me a note in the post box, and I'll get back in touch.'

'I wish I was coming to London with you, where are you staying.'

'I'm staying with Jane Rolands and her family, you don't know them.'

''Well tell me all about it when you come back.'

'I will John,' his bleeper went, must get to a phone,' he said, 'bye for now Nurse Spencer.' and with a smile he was gone.

Back on the ward Julie was greeted by the sound of crying babies. You can always tell when it's feed time she said to herself and after having a word with her junior she went into the kitchen to prepare the bottles. Carefully levelling off the dried milk scoops she put them into the clean measuring jug and added the boiling water. She then took the sterilised bottles and poured the required amount into each bottle and cooled it off to the right temperature. Picking up one of the babies as she got back to the ward her maternal instincts were awakened and she lovingly cradled the little girl who had been admitted with meningitis. Julie liked working with children, they were so genuine in their response to illness. It

Just as it Was

sometimes upset her greatly to see the procedures which sometimes had to be carried out on the children. Injections and lumbar punctures were two of the things which regularly had to be done on the medical ward and they brought out a deep feeling of protectiveness in her. She had not had much experience with very small children and babies but she found that she had a love of the work and it was so rewarding to see them going home healthily after treatment. One day she thought I'll have children of my own, but that's a long way off, there's a lot to do first. 'This is your last day before your holiday isn't it?' Nurse Foster had finished feeding the baby that she was holding and was in the process of changing his nappy. 'Yes and I'm ready for it.'

'Well enjoy yourself, where are you going?'

'I'm going to London, to stay with friends.'

'Ooh I've never been to London, I'd love to go. I'd like to visit all those places that people talk about, Buckingham palace and the Tower and London bridge.'

'I'm going to visit the family of a girl who I made friends with when I first came onto the wards here. She lost a leg in the train crash and she was only sixteen as I was at the time. I've kept in touch with her by letters but I don't really know what to expect. She's able to work now and she's got an office job in an insurance company.'

'Crikey, poor girl, what a rotten thing to happen, losing a leg at sixteen.'

'It was, but she seems to be getting on with her life, her parents were wonderful people and they've encouraged her to

Just as it Was

do all sorts of things, I can't wait to see them all again. Just a few hours now and then I'll be on my way.'

'I've put some groceries in this bag for Mrs Rolands. A tin of salmon some sugar and biscuits and things, she'll have an extra mouth to feed and you can't go eating all their rations.'

'Oh thanks Mum.' Julie was standing in the passageway with her Mum and Dad as they were waving her off on her journey to the big city.

'Just keep your eyes open and watch your purse when you're out and about,' her father gave her a hug and a kiss along with his word of warning. Crikey, I bet Dad thinks Fagin and his boys are still roaming the London streets. 'I'll be careful Dad.'

'And here, put this in your purse.' Mr Spencer thrust a five pound note into his daughter's hand, be careful with it, you'll need something to spend when you go out and you can buy a bit of something for Mrs Rolands for looking after you. Now put it in your handbag where it's safe and don't go throwing it about.'

'Oh Dad,' Julie didn't know what to say, she knew that it must have taken her Dad weeks to save the money and she hadn't expected it.

'Go on now, you're going to miss your train if you don't look sharp.'

Julie picked up her case and stepped out into the street, the two waved her off until she was out of sight.

Just as it Was

There were little groups of people waiting for the train and it wasn't long before it came chugging into the platform letting out steam as the brakes juddered it to a halt. Doors were flung open and some of the people who alighted were greeted and embraced by others as the waiting travellers climbed into the carriages. Julie moved along the corridor looking for suitable companions, seeing a middle-aged couple she decided that this was the one and she walked in. 'Here, let me lift that case up for you it looks heavy.' The man smiled at her as he put her case on the luggage rack.

'Are you going far?' his wife turned towards Julie.'

'I'm going to London.'

'So are we have you been before?'

'Once with my family, just for the day.'

'Nice.' said the woman. Julie didn't know whether to take out her book which she had intended to catch up with on the journey or if perhaps it would look unfriendly. She decided against it. All the carriage doors were banged shut and as the guard blew his whistle the train moved slowly forward with much hissing and creaking.

'We're off now, there's plenty of room on the train, not many people travelling today' the woman settled back more comfortably in her seat looking directly at Julie, ready for conversation. This is going to be interesting, Julie thought, I should have brought my Mum and Dad with me. The next question wasn't long in coming. 'Are you staying long this time?'

Just as it Was

'I'll get no peace until I give her chapter and verse and so Julie told the couple of how she had met the Roland family and of the purpose of her visit. The journey passed quickly, there was hardly a lull in the conversation and by the time that the train reached King's Cross station Julie knew all about the previous visits of Ken and Mavis Stott to London and they were familiar with the reason for her visit. 'Well here we are, let me get your case down for you, and have a lovely time with your friend young lady, you never know we might bump into you in the West-End.'

Crikey, you might, if I ever get there Julie thought. She didn't think that her funds would stretch to that though how far did your money go in London. Mr and Mrs Stott bid her goodbye and she made her way through the ticket barrier and into the street.

Suddenly the world had gone mad, Julie was thrust into a world of human beings scurrying to their chosen destination. Thronged masses drove Julie forward in a state of complete wonder. Where were they all going? The men with bowler hats and rolled umbrellas and women wearing the latest Dior fashion. Everyone moving as though there wasn't a minute to spare, busy, important business ahead of them it seemed.

'Hello Julie' it's lovely to see you.'

Julie looked in amazement at the pretty sun tanned female whom she recognised as Jane from the photographs that she had received. There was no evidence of the trauma she had suffered, and since the almost three years when they first met

Just as it Was

Jane had grown into a confident and stylish young woman. 'Jane, I'm here at last, oh, I'm so excited to see you and to be in London, you look absolutely smashing.'

'Thanks' Jane laughed, 'and so do you. Come on we've got to take a taxi, Dad's using the car today so he couldn't bring me to meet you but they're all really looking forward to seeing you again.' The girls made their way out of the station and to the taxi rank where Jane hailed a cab she gave the name of her road,' it's off 'Latchmere Rd' she called to the driver and ushering Julie into the back seat Jane expertly lifted her legs into the car and they drove off towards the Roland's home. Julie was fascinated, the traffic was heavy and as they travelled she caught glimpses of small shops. Delicatessens with a marked foreign appearance and dress shops the likes of which she had never seen before. Jewellers shops's dazzling lights which excited and encouraged passers by to take a look at the beautiful things that they could buy. In sharp contrast separating these consumer dreams occasionally clumps of damaged buildings left over from the onslaught of the blitz only a few years back were a stark reminder of the recent history of London. Clapham Junction, Lavender Rd. familiar names which now became realities and at last they pulled up outside Jane's home. Carrying her case and walking behind Jane Julie entered the front door and was immediately drawn into Mrs Roland's arms. 'Oh we've all so looked forward to seeing you again, we thought it would never happen.' She released the girl and held her at arms length. 'You look a bit pale, have they been working you too hard, nursing is such a tough job, I don't know how you do it. You're angels all of

Just as it Was

you, and we'll never forget what you and the doctors did for Jane.' Julie didn't know what to say so she took the small parcel of groceries that her Mum had sent and handed them to Jane's Mum. 'I hope these 'll come in useful, it's not much but my my mother insisted that I bring something.'

'That was very kind of your Mum, we still have to queue for extras sometimes so thank you very much I appreciate what you've brought, you tell your Mum that; come on now Gran's in the front room she's dying to meet you so when you've taken your coat off and taken your case upstairs Jane 'll show the way.'

Julie followed her friend up the narrow stairs noticing how well Jane managed them, obviously she didn't move as easily as others but the way that she coped and didn't make a trial of her artificial leg was amazing. Julie followed her into a medium sized room with two single beds ranged along the long wall side by side. 'Just pop your things down and we'll go down and meet Gran you can hang your things up later if that's O.K. with you.'

Oh dear, this was all so different, Yorkshire was such a long way away and Julie was suddenly very aware that she was completely alone amongst strangers, it was the first time that she had been away from her family and a little feeling of homesickness swept over her, it was all so strange and Doncaster seemed a million miles away at that moment. 'I'd like to pop into the bathroom.'

Just as it Was

Well we've just had a bath put into the small bedroom, if you want to use the toilet though it's downstairs next to the coal-house.'

'Oh I just want to freshen up a bit, I'll be ready to come down in a few minutes.'

It didn't take Julie long and led by Jane they entered the front room together. It was a homely room with a small fireplace set into a tiled chimney place with brass fire irons and a fender lending a finishing touch to the hearth. There was a carpet square and a small three piece suite and in one of the chairs there sat an elderly lady who appeared to be in her late seventies or eighties. 'Well bless my soul, here you are at last, I thought I'd never live long enough to see you and I've 'eard so much about you.' She took her stick in her right hand and pushing herself up on the chair arm she took a step towards Julie. 'I'm Grandma Rolands, the family call me Grannie Flo among other things and you're welcome to do the same if you like.' She peered up at Julie, 'you're just as pretty as they said you was now come and let me 'ave a good look at you, I ain't seen many Yorkshire folk but I've 'eard a lot about 'em.'

'I've been wanting to come to see Jane and all of you for along time, but Dad thought I wasn't old enough 'til now, he's a bit strict.'

'Nothing wrong with that, and you was both a bit young when all that business with the train crash 'appened, but y'ere 'ere now and I 'ope yer both going to enjoy yerselves. Jane's got a few days off and there's plenty to do around here and the

Just as it Was

weather's nice. She's been looking forward to showing you around.' Jane instantly took to the old lady, her own grandparents had been dead long before she was born and it was nice to meet Jane's Grandmother and just for a little while perhaps it would be an enjoyable experience to be part of a family who had a grandmother. 'There's a good picture on at the cinema, you could go there tonight if you wanted to, there's two of you you'd be safe enough.'

'That's a good idea Gran, perhaps we will.'

Mrs Rolands came through from the kitchen, 'if you'd like to come through I've put out something to eat, just a biting on we'll be having a proper meal when Dad comes home this evening.'

'Would you like to have a walk in Battersea Park?'

'It's a lovely afternoon, I think that would be nice.'

'O.K., I've just to have a look at the hamster, we're looking after him until cousin Philip comes back from holiday, they only live a few doors away, Auntie Edna, Uncle Billie and Phil he's seven and he thinks the world of 'Rory', that's what he calls the hamster.'

'Oh I'll come and have a look at him.' Julie followed her friend to the little porch which was through the back door and led onto the small garden she heard a shriek from Jane. 'Oh! where's Rory, the cage's empty' Mrs Rolands heard the cry and she came running through with an anxious look on her face. 'How has it happened the door's open, where on earth can he be?'

Just as it Was

'Anywhere between here and Buckingham palace' said Gran who had come out to see what the fuss was about.'

'Rory, Rory, come Rory,' they searched the garden and the house and all the surrounding area but there was no sign of the little fella. When Mr Rolands came home they all ate their meal and then resumed the search extending it to neighbours' homes and gardens but not a sign of the hamster. Evening drifted into night, the plans of going to the cinema had been put back and it was with heavy hearts that they all went to bed. How could they break the news to little Philip about the disappearance of his pet. Grandma went up to bed before the others and as Jane and Julie were settling down to sleep they chatted for a while discussing the events of the day and hoping that perhaps when they awoke Rory would have crawled back to his cage. Silence descended upon the house and all slept deeply until screams which chilled the marrow came from Gran's room. 'Everyone rushed to her aid and the poor old lady was in a state of shock. 'Somethings crawled all over me, I felt something creeping up me nightie, what is it, what is it?' she yelled out.

'You're O'K Mum, there's no one here.'

'I can still feel it, pull the clothes back whatever is it? get it orf me.'

Mrs Rolands pulled off the bedclothes and they were all amazed to see the bottom of Grans nightie nibbled away and a sudden movement as a small furry creature fell out of her bed.

Just as it Was

'Quick shut the bedroom door, Rory's in here, he's been in bed with gran' Jane called.

The old lady recovered herself very quickly, she sat up and looked around, 'where is he, the little beggar, it's the first time I've shared me bed with a flaming hamster, and look at me nightie, it's me best nightie.'

'Gran, we'll buy you another nightie, thank goodness we've found the hamster , Phil need never know anything about this.' The relief on Jane's face was tangible, but by the look on her grandmother's face she knew that the tale of the hamster would be told for a very long time to come.

Just as it Was

18

Out And About In London

'Shall we go into the city today?'

'I'd like that, could we visit the tower?'

'There's a tour bus if you fancy that.' Julie was only too ready to fall in with the idea of taking the bus tour she had seen how well Jane coped with her artificial leg but she was sure that there would be plenty of walking to do during the day and a bus tour seemed the ideal thing. 'Don't worry about the dishes girls.' Mrs Rolands was happy to see the two girls getting on so well together. Although they had written to each other occasionally they had only met over a hospital bed before and it was good to see that they were enjoying each others company. 'Thanks for breakfast Mrs Rolands.'

'What about lunch are you going to eat with us when you get back?'

'We can get a meal in London today can't we? you must know somewhere, Jane.'

'Perhaps we can go to the Lyons House in Picadilly.'

'Just as you like, you both look very nice anyway, Mrs Rolands looked at the girls admiringly. Julie was wearing a full skirted dress which showed off her tiny waist and with it's eye catching colourful large dots on the white background she was

183

Just as it Was

sure to draw peoples attention. Jane had her hair fashioned in the latest bubble cut style and she was wearing a long full skirt with a very fetching top which showed off her girlish figure very prettily.

'You girls watch out you'll have the lads after you.' Gran had recovered from her ordeal of the night before and she looked up from her newspaper as the girls said their goodbyes and made for the tube station. 'Are you O.K. Jane?' the girls had arrived on the platform waiting for the tube which would take them to Piccadilly. 'I'm fine, we'll have to make a push though there's plenty waiting to get on.' As the train pulled in there was a rush forward and as she lifted her leg to board the tube someone caught Jane on the shoulder causing her to lose her balance. 'Look out' Julie turned impatiently on the offender.

'I'm so sorry, I didn't mean to push, your friend just went over, is she alright now?'

'No thanks to you,' Julie looked into the face of the young man who had spoken, he looked genuinely concerned. 'Look I didn't mean to push her over, she just toppled.' By this time Jane had found a seat and with a withering look at the young man Julie left and went to sit near to her friend. 'Are you o.k. Jane?'

'Yes course I am, I wouldn't mind bumping into him again.'

Julie looked over to where the boy was sitting, he was deep in conversation with another lad of about the same age and as she looked away she felt that there were looks coming their way from the other two. 'Do you have a boyfriend at the moment Julie?'

Just as it Was

'Well I am sort of going out with someone, not really a boy friend, how about you?'

'I've met one or two boys at the youth club, and there was a lad from the office who I went out with a few times but it's taken me such a long time to learn to get around that I haven't really been able to go out and about much.'

'Do you like working in the office?'

'Oh yes but that's another thing, I had to go to night school to learn typing and shorthand it took a lot of my time up.' In no time at all the tube arrived at Piccadilly station, as the girls got off the train they saw the two lads waiting a few yards away and on seeing them the boys walked up to them. 'Look I'm awfully sorry, I really didn't mean to push you over.'

'It's not your fault' Jane looked straight at the young man, 'I find it hard to balance on one leg sometimes.' The lad looked very uncomfortable, he didn't know what to say, 'you mean?'

'Yes I lost my leg in a train accident three years ago, I easily topple.'

'I had no idea, you seemed really up for it and just one of the crowd.'

'That's how I want to look, but sometimes it doesn't quite work.'

'Well I am sorry, and I hope that you're alright now.'

'Perfectly' said Jane and with that they all made their way out onto the street.

'Here's the tour bus now' the girls had bought their tickets from the kiosk and they got aboard and waited for the bus to

Just as it Was

fill up. The day was fine and everyone wore cotton dresses and blouses and the men were in slacks and open necked sports shirts. The upper deck had filled up first everyone wanting the best vantage point for viewing but with the guide ready to give his running commentary the two girls were sitting chatting on the lower deck.

'Look who's just got on the bus' Jane nudged her friend she was just in time to see the two lads who had been on the train climbing up the stairs of the bus. 'Can't get away from them can we?' The driver climbed into his cab and with a rev of his engine the tour of London began. Julie was thrilled to see wonderful sights of the great city and as the guide extolled about the history of the Tower, and the Parliament buildings and the various other historic buildings she was overwhelmed by the beauty of the city. The bridges in their glory associated with films which she had seen and poetry which she had read were brought to life. The monuments and the venerated buildings, shops which were internationally famous and famous hospitals Guys and, St Thomas and many, many other landmarks. Of course there was also the bomb damage, there was still a lot of restoration to be done. Jane gazed out of the window silently no doubt thinking about the times when she had ventured out independently as a child on two legs, accompanied by her parents of course. She turned to Julie now 'what do you think then?'

'It's wonderful, everyone should see London, after all that bombing during the war and what the people went through in the blitz I think it's a miracle the way that it looks today.'

Just as it Was

'Yes the blitz was terrible nearly everybody suffered from losing relatives one way or another during the war.'

'Battersea was badly hit wasn't it.'

'Yes, my Dad lost his sister and her family in a bombing raid in 1940. They were all in the house and there was a direct hit. Aunty Peggy Uncle Wilf and my cousins Valerie and Ron all killed.'

'Oh Jane,' Julie took her hand and squeezed it, it must have been hell. We had a few raids in Doncaster and people were killed, but the bombs dropped on London, it doesn't bear thinking about.'

'No and that's the last that we're going to say about it,' Jane lifted her chin up and looked out of the window as the bus stopped. People were alighting and she saw the two boys standing on the pavement looking directly at her through the bus window. 'I think someone's waiting for us,' she said to Julie. To avoid the crush Jane and Julie were almost the last two to get off the bus. 'It seems that we were meant to meet today, I'm Duncan and this is Michael, we couldn't believe our eyes when we saw you two on the tour bus.' The boys smiled warmly and waited for the response. Before Julie could say anything Jane smiled broadly and said 'my horoscope said that I was in for an interesting day so this must be it.'

'It could be, we're in London for the week during the summer vacation, we're just sightseeing and having a break from uni.'

'You're not Londoners then?'

'No we're in our second year at Warwickshire, I'm reading English and Michael's studying History.'

Just as it Was

'This is the place to do it, you can enjoy and study at the same time.'

'We don't know our way around London very well, we could do with someone to help us.'

All this time Julie kept quiet, she could see the mutual interest between Jane and Duncan and she wasn't going to spoil it for her. 'What do you think Julie, should we take pity on these two lost young men?'

'Well since I'm from Yorkshire and just as much lost in London as them it's entirely up to you Jane.'

'O.K. Where's it to be Westminster Abbey and Poet's corner or The Tower and the Kings and Queens of England.'

Michael interrupted 'well if you don't mind I'm a bit peckish I would like some lunch if you know somewhere where the food is good and plentiful and the price isn't too high.'

'Don't worry about that we'll pay for ourselves' Julie was not going to be under any obligation to these two, they had only just met and they needed to be vetted.

'Lets go to Lyons in Piccadilly, the service and the food are excellent.'

'Come on then I'm hungry' They found a table and their order was soon taken by one of the nippies. The restaurant was pleasantly full with tourists and shoppers and others who were on their break from the office and the relaxed atmosphere was picked up by the youngsters who chatted away easily. 'This looks good,' full plates of sausage egg and chips were placed in front of them and then a pot of tea and fancy cakes

Just as it Was

which were soon demolished. 'That's better, I was really hungry,' Michael took the last cake from the plate after making sure that no-one else wanted it. 'What now then?' they all looked at Jane.

'We could take a look at the British Library or The Houses of Parliament.' There didn't seem to be much enthusiasm for that so she looked around the group playfully' or we could take a look at Buckingham palace and then because the weather is so fine we could make our way to the park, a small cheer went up from the others. As they left The Lyons Corner House Duncan took Jane's arm and they walked on ahead as Michael and Julie fell in behind them. 'You're a long way from Yorkshire.'

'Yes I'm spending a week with Jane's family, I met them when Jane was a patient in hospital after a train crash. I'd just begun my nursing career and because we were the same age we had a lot in common and I suppose that's why we became friends.'

'She's a wonderful girl so full of life.'

'Yes just look at her now, she seems to be hitting it off with Duncan, they're getting on like a house on fire.'

'He's a great guy, he'd go out of his way for anyone, but I've never known him pay so much attention to a girl before, just look at them chatting away,I think they've forgotten all about us.'

'Jane deserves happiness, I'm glad they're getting on so well, she's having a lovely day.'

'And what about you.'

Just as it Was

'I think that London is great, I'm really a country lover at heart, but there's something for everyone here as far as I can see.'

'Yes.' said the young man looking at her out of the corner of his eye. The crowd around the palace had their cameras out and they were taking pictures of the guards who stood in their sentry boxes like tin soldiers, not a twitch as some of the crowd did their best to distract them. People of many nationalities were drawn by the spectacle and Julie marvelled at the beauty, grandeur and history that was part of this vibrant and wonderful city and she felt herself falling under it's spell. There were many other attractions for the tourists to snap including the Victoria memorial and the palace itself with the balcony from which the King and Queen and their family waved on Royal occasions. The sense of occasion was tangible as the Union Jack fluttered from the standard and as a large black Daimler swept out of the gates the crowd surged forward only to see that it was an official on his way about his business. 'This place was bombed during the war wasn't it?' Julie recalled seeing film at the cinema of King George and Queen Elizabeth moving among crowds from the east End of London and sharing some of their experiences.

'Yes the chapel was destroyed, there was damage to some of the palace windows as well, but thank goodness it's still here.' Michael obviously knew his stuff about the war.

'Jane's family live in Battersea and they had some of their family killed in the bombing, poor girl, she's gone through a lot.' Jane called to them, 'time we were moving on let's make

Just as it Was

our way into the park, St Jame's Park, we can cool off in there I'm so hot.'

'Lead on you're a great guide,' Julie caught up with her friend and Duncan dropped back to speak with Michael. 'You two are getting on well, what do think to him?' Jane asked.

'He's been telling me about his family, his Mum was a nurse at Great Ormond St. before she married. We've been talking about hospitals would you believe, and he now knows all about me and you and Doncaster.'

'There's a nurse in his family then?'

'Well yes, she's not working now but Great Ormond St, it must have been exciting to be part of that and to live in London.'

'Would you like to work in one of the London Hospitals?'

'Well I might, I've taken quite a fancy to it, London is such a magnificent place, history oozing out of every brick it really is wonderful.'

'Nothing to keep you in Doncaster then no serious boyfriend yet so you said?'

'I've to pass my finals first then who knows what will happen.'

'Julie you haven't answered my question.'

'Oh about a serious boyfriend, there's someone who I am very fond of but I don't think that it'll work.'

'Why not is he a different religion?'

'No Jane it's a matter of class.'

'Not a dukes son?'

Just as it Was

'Don't be daft, he's a doctor and his parents are very wealthy and upper class.'

'Oh well, I know what you mean, don't get obove your station this class system of ours; but you could fit in anywhere Julie!'

'He wants me to meet them but oh, I don't know well I do actually, he's so nice but we're just friends at the moment.'

The boys caught up with them as they reached the Park, 'wow this is lovely, look at the size of the lake it's huge, so big and everything looks so fresh and green after being among the crowds. What a treat let's sit under one of these big shady trees.'

'Come on there's a bench under this tree we can sit here and rest for a bit and cool off.'

Julie brought out a bag of toffees which she had bought and she passed them around. 'Hey we can't eat your sweet ration,' Duncan laughed but still he reached for a toffee.

'I,ve been saving my coupons up, it's a treat,' she responded.

'Fancy the war's over and we still have shortages it's so tough this rationing, foods still a bit scarce but at least we see oranges and bananas again sometimes. And did you see the queues as we passed on the bus, things are still tight, people still join on the end of a queue whatever it's for hoping for a treat.'

'My dad doesn't, he doesn't believe in queueing, it gets him into trouble sometimes, especially when people are waiting for buses.'

Just as it Was

'Your Dad sounds like a character, we conform too easily in England.'

'I don't know about that , he makes me blush sometimes' Julie retorted.

'I like girls who blush,' Michael smiled at her she just smiled back sweetly and turned to her friend. 'And what about you Jane have you had enough? you've really shown us the sights of London today.'

'Oh there's plenty more to see, there's things in this city that I haven't seen yet.'

'Well how about meeting up again and having a look at more of London?'

'I'm fine with that' Duncan joined in 'how about you girls?' I've really enjoyed today,'

'Me too, whatever you want to do,' if Jane doesn't mind showing us more of London I'm all for it' Julie looked towards her friend.

'Well I have plans for tomorrow, can we make it Thursday?'

'Same place, same time Thursday then.'

'It's been a super day thank you Jane for showing us the sights, I can't believe our luck meeting you girls the way that we did.' Duncan took her hand and thanked her again. 'See you Thursday then.'

The girls had the house to themselves when they arrived home. Mum and Gran weren't yet back from the market and

Just as it Was

Jane's father hadn't got in from work. The evening meal was prepared and cooking slowly in the side oven and all that was left to do was to set the table. The girls were pleased to see Rory happily playing on his wheel apparently the memory of his escape to freedom was a thing of the past. They made themselves a cup of tea and each sat in a chair by the fireplace. 'What did you think to Duncan then you seemed to have a lot to talk about?'

'I like Duncan, he has a great sense of humour and he loves to read.'

'That's just as well seeing that it's his subject' Jane laughed.

'He likes the theatre and music as well.'

'What sort of music, concerts and things?'

'He used to sing in a choir, stuff like Vaughn Williams and show stuff some of Sigmund Romburg's choruses and Leonard Bernstein, he thought that I might like to go to a concert with him sometime.'

'Do you like music?'

'I do but I haven't been to anything like that, more like Frank Sinatra on film although I did hear Donald Peers once perhaps I could give the concert a go.'

'You'll have to tell your Mum and Dad about him.'

'They'll want me to bring him home, we'll have to see how it goes.'

'What kind of a family does he come from, did he talk about them?'

Just as it Was

'He did a bit, quite ordinary I think, Duncan won a scholarship to university and he hopes to go on to teach.'

'Well I'm glad you like him, and thanks Jane, thanks so much for inviting me to London and for showing me all the lovely places that we've seen today, I'll have plenty to talk about and think about when I get back to Doncaster.'

'I hope you'll come again Julie.'

'I will, London has made a big impression on me I love it.'

Jane and Julie met Duncan and Michael several times during the next week and each time Jane and Duncan seemed to become more and more close. Duncan was anxious not to challenge her too much physically and his consideration for her never wavered. They were on such an understanding of each other, there was so much to talk about, so many interests shared that her ability to walk long distances seemed not to matter. Today Jane and Julie were spending a day together without the boys. The summery weather had made them decide to pack a picnic basket and take it into Battersea park. They were taking a day off from sightseeing and as they went along Cherry Tree Walk Julie exclaimed her wonder at their surroundings. 'How wonderful, it's like finding an oasis in the desert.'

'We often come in here, I know just the place for a picnic.' Jane laughed at her friend 'I can't promise any camels though.' Julie took her arm and they arrived at a spot where there was an inviting bench seat under a tree 'here we are' the girls settled themselves down and took out the sandwiches and cakes and poured themselves drinks from the

Just as it Was

Thermos Flask. The sun blazed down on them and as they finished the meal and began to chat Julie packed away the leftovers and the rubbish.' 'It's been so good of you come to see me Julie.'

'What do you mean, I'd have been here before now if my parents hadn't thought that I was too young to travel on my own.'

'But spending your holiday with somebody like me I can't get about like you, I can't go dancing or play tennis or anything like that.'

'Jane I've had; am having a wonderful time your family are terrific and you are an absolutely fantastic girl I've completely fallen in love with London thanks to you for showing me around.'

'Well meeting Duncan and Michael has helped and I would never have met them if it wasn't for you.'

'Surely you get out and about with your friends?'

'My friends are all courting now, it's difficult for them to arrange a blind date for a girl with only one leg. Don't get me wrong Julie I'm not feeling sorry for myself, I'm just telling it like it is.'

'I suppose that there are things that you can't do and it's easy for me to talk, but you have so much to offer.'

'Oh yea, such as?'

'You're a very attractive girl with a lively mind and a sense of fun, I think that Duncan's very taken with you.'

Just as it Was

'Well I quite like him, in fact I can't wait to see him again, I doubt that it will go very far though, time will tell. What about you, you mentioned that there was somebody.'

'Oh he's great, John Gibson, he's a houseman and he's taken me out a few times.'

'Well a Dr and Nurse romance that's nice.'

'Well it wouldn't be so bad if his parents weren't so upper class, he wants to take me to meet them but it's not going to work. I couldn't take him to our house.'

'Why what do you mean?'

'Well you've heard of Ebb and Flo, that's my Mum and Dad. They're the salt of the earth but John's parents are more like the duke and duchess. Their family all had public school educations and they move in exalted circles, my parents love fish and chips and Dad likes the White Swan and a pint of best bitter.'

'But we're all human beings Julie.'

'Yes and we've all been divided by birth, we are what we are.'

'You could get on anywhere with anybody I know you could.'

'Perhaps I could but I'm not going to leave my family behind and anyway I'm not sure of my feelings for John Gibson. I'm flattered of course, but I have felt the same way about other people.'

'You used to talk about Colin in your letters.'

'Yes I was very fond of Colin but I haven't heard from him for some time now, he's still up in Richmond as far as I know.'

Just as it Was

'Oh Julie, I suppose it'll all sort itself out sooner or later, we never know what might happen.'

'All I know at the moment Jane is that I'm going to have another of those lovely butterfly buns that your Gran made, come on let's get a bit of sunbathing in.'

Back at the house they found the rest of the family sitting out in the small back garden. They had taken folding chairs out there and Gran was sittng with her dress hitched up over her knees and a big straw hat on her head. The intense heat had gone out of the day but a heavy sultry atmosphere hung over Battersea. 'I'm melting away, I can't stand it like I used to, I can't put me bathing costume on it'd scare the birds away' they all laughed.

'Did you ever have a costume Gran?'

'Me 'ave a costume, I'll say I did, it had a little skirt and it was made outta wool course I 'ad to be careful where I wore it. Your grand-dad weren't keen on it, specially after we got courting.'

'Was he jealous Gran?'

'I don't know about that, perhaps embarrassed were a better way of describing it, things was different in our day.' She gave a little laugh, the girls loved to hear her stories and again Julie wished that she had known her own grandmother. Granny Flo was an important part of the family and they all loved and respected her. 'You going back to Yorkshire tomorrow Julie?'

'Yes, and I wish that I could stay longer.'

Just as it Was

'We've loved having you and I hope that you'll come back again.' Mrs Rolands got out of her chair, 'I've got some fresh orange juice in the pantry, who'd like some.'

'I'll help you Mrs Rolands' the two went into the house as Dad and Gran listened to Jane's story of her afternoon in Battersea park. It was so comforting sitting there in the garden as evening slowly fell around them. In the midst of the family Julie felt as though she belonged and her experience of London had given her a taste for the capital and she wanted to see more of it. She was sure that she would come back. 'I'm taking you to the railway station tomorrow, you'll be coming with us wont you Jane?'

'Course I will Dad, it'll be nice to get a lift though.'

'Thanks Mr Rolands,I better go and get my packing done,' Julie felt sad about leaving her new friends although she had missed her own family. It had been strange as well, being away from the hospital and her colleagues, and John what was she going to do about him, The life she had left behind for a little while had to be taken up again and it was with mixed feelings that she climbed the stairs to the bedroom.

The three of them arrived on the platform in good time to catch the train to Doncaster. There were just a few people about and as she caught a glimpse of two familiar figures approaching, as they got closer Julie recognised Duncan and Michael. 'Couldn't let you leave without saying goodbye.' Michael smiled at Julie and handed her some magazines. 'For you to look at on your journey, thanks it's been great

Just as it Was

discovering parts of London with you perhaps we'll do it again sometime.'

'Are you going to introduce me to these two young men?' Mr Rowlands interrupted.

'Course Dad, we told you about Duncan and Michael, I forgot that you hadn't met them.'

The boys shook hands with Mr Rolands and Duncan said, 'if it's alright with you sir I'd like to take Jane to a concert when I come to London next time and I'd like to write to her.'

'Young man you better ask Jane about that, she has a mind of her own,' he looked over at his daughter and he knew from the happy look on her face what the answer would be.

The announcement came over the station tannoy that the train for Edinburgh, stopping at Peterborough, Sheffeld, and Doncaster was now ready for boarding and Julie said a tearful goodbye to her friends. She hugged Jane warmly and promised that she would be back before too long. As the train moved away she lowered the window of the carriage and waved to the others before settling back in her seat. The events of the past week were imprinted on her mind and she recalled the outings that she had shared with Jane and the boys and the warmth of the family and how they had readily accepted her as one of them. They had coped so well with the accident that had befallen Jane and she was so pleased that she had been able to keep her promise to visit them and she had a very strong feeling that she certainly would go back there again.

Just as it Was

Just as it Was

19

After London

'Nurse you can go to first dinner. This afternoon we're to pull the beds out and do the high sweeping.' Sister Newton smiled as she spoke to Julie.

'Yes Sister.' High sweeping, it was a job that she disliked and she wondered what on earth it had to do with nurse training. The long handled brushes which extended up to the high ceilings were unwieldy and as far as she was concerned useless. This was not why she had become a nurse and resentment built within her. However she had to do as she was told and after coming back onto the ward after first lunch she and Nurse Foster pulled the beds into the middle of the ward and took turns with the high sweeping brush. Foster paused after an energetic spurt and took a deep breath, 'wow, I'll have to stop for a bit,' she leant onto the end of one of the beds, as she put down her brush and asked Julie, 'well, did you enjoy London?'

'It was wonderful, I'd like to be back there.'

'Would you really, but you haven't finished your training yet.'

Just as it Was

'I know, I really must get the books out and get some studying done, it's my last year and I'll soon be taking my finals. I'll have to get down to some serious revision.'

'You'll get through, what are you going to do after you're qualified?'

'I don't exactly know I expect I'll look for a staff nurse's post, I'd like female surgical.'

'I want to train to be a midwife, that's if I ever get through my exams.'

'Well come on let's put a bit more effort into this high sweeping,' Julie laughed, 'we might get a question on it, you never know.' Later in the day Julie popped her head around sister's office door. 'Reporting off duty sister.'

'Oh Nurse Spencer it's nice to have you back, I haven't had a chance to ask you about your holiday, did you have a good time in London?'

'Yes thank you sister.'

'I trained in London you know,' she fiddled with the pen which she was using to fill out the treatment book.

'I didn't know that but I do envy you I really liked the place.'

'Well London was wonderful, it was a teaching hospital though and the medical students almost fell over themselves to do the procedures. There's a lot to be said for training at a hospital like this one the nurses get a lot more hands on experience.'

'Even so being in London must have been really good.'

Just as it Was

'It was and it seems to have made a big impression on you Nurse Spencer, I'm glad that you enjoyed it.'

After going into the cloakroom to take off her cap and apron and put on her gabardine and veil Julie decided to slip into the dining room to see if there was any mail in her post box. She took out the small envelope that she found there and popped it into her bag , she would wait until she reached home to see what it said.

The living room was full of people as Julie arrived home her sister was visiting and the news was exciting. Mum was absolutely beaming and Dad was sitting in his wooden armchair pretending to concentrate on his newspaper but nevertheless listening to every word. Doris was smiling happily as she told her sister, 'what do you think, great news Babs is having a baby we're are going to be aunts and our John's going to be an uncle,isn't it great.'

'What! Babs is having a baby, that's wonderful, we haven't had a baby in this family for years what about that Mam, you and Dad Grandma and Granddad.' Julie went over to her eldest sister who had only just arrived and who was grinning broadly, it's true, there's a long way to go yet.' The irrepressible Doris continued to celebrate the news 'we're going to have a little baby in the family, I can't wait to tell my workmates.' Julie went over to her sister and put her arms around her. 'Oh sis, how wonderful, how are you feeling?'

Just as it Was

Babs smiled, 'very happy' then she pulled a face 'a bit grotty in the mornings though, and I can't look at a cup of tea without feeling squeasy.'

'Oh that'll pass, and just think the first baby in the family since John, it will feel strange, we'll all have to brush up on our baby skills'.

'There's plenty of us to spoil him, or her.' Mrs Spencer although delighted at the thought of becoming a grandmother at last was anxious that her strict routine shouldn't be disrupted there were meals to get ready and other chores to see to. 'I've just made a pot of tea Julie if you want one, I'm off upstairs now to finish cleaning the windows inside.'

'Thanks Mum I'll just take my coat and things off.' After hanging them in the passageway she slipped into the front room and opened up the letter.

DearJulie,

I hope that you enjoyed your holiday in London and that you are now safely back here. I have missed you and missed the outings which we have been taking together and I am very much looking forward to seeing you again. About the dinner dance, it is arranged for the second Saturday in September, I have told my parents that I would like to take you to meet them and they are anxious that I should do that. The dress is formal but I know that wont be a problem for you. Do say that you will come, I am letting you know in good time so that you can arrange your off duty. The hospital hasn't been the same

Just as it Was

without you around, not for me anyway. Please let me know about the dance. I'll look for your letter in the post box.

With love

John.

She folded the note put it in her pocket and went back into the living room to join the rest of her family where Doris and Babs were setting the table for tea. Mrs Spencer having finished her chores came downstairs. 'You're having something to eat with us Barbara we're having mussels and oven bottom cakes, I made them this afternoon and they're lovely and fresh, what do you think?'

'I'd love some of your home baking Mum but I'll pass on the mussels, and if you've got some orange juice I'll have that instead of tea please.' The girls carried on taking out the assorted crockery from the kitchen cupboard setting the table as Mrs Spencer buttered the bread and brought through the dish of mussels which had been brought from the market that afternoon and boiled and prepared by Mr Spencer, this was his territory and he didn't trust any other member of the family to do it properly. As they drew up the chairs to the table Dad put on the home service to listen to the news. The five of them sat companionably together enjoying the food and the news which Babs had brought about the next generation of their family. Later Doris was going over to see some friends and Babs and Julie volunteered to do the washing up. 'There's no hot water, I'll have to boil the kettle' Julie fetched the kettle through from the fireplace and filled it

Just as it Was

with water and put it on the gas ring. The sisters waited for it to boil. 'I don't see much of you these days Julie.'

'No, well I have been away for a week.'

'And before that, what have you been doing have you been getting out much.'

Julie suspected that this conversation was leading somewhere. 'What's Mum told you?'

'A few weeks ago she told me that you were seeing one of the Doctors at the hospital, going out with him.'

'Oh Babs, I have, only once or twice.'

'Mum's a bit upset about it, in fact she's not happy at all, she used to like Colin you know and so did Dad are you still seeing him this doctor.'

'We're just friends he would like it to be more and he's asked me to meet his parents, there's a dinner dance being held by his father's organization and he wants me to go with him to meet them.'

Babs gave her sister a sideways look. 'Are you going?'

'I haven't given him an answer yet.'

'How serious is it?'

'I like him, he's more serious than me but I enjoy going out with him, I'm not sure, I don't know how I feel.'

'Julie you're just nineteen, you'll fall in love many times yet.'

Julie laughed. 'Oh I already have, the lad who had the lesson after mine at the music classes when I was thirteen, the lad in

Just as it Was

the grocer's shop, and Eric Portman the film star, I was head over heels about him, I don't know whether I'm in love with John though, I think I'm afraid to be. Come on Babs forget about it.'

'That's all well and good but you might get hurt, what do his family do where does his father work?'

'He's got an important position in a bank a very important position.'

'And our Dad's a labourer can you imagine the conversations between them, she mimicked her father 'did you have a bet in the two-thirty then Charlie?''

Julie had to laugh at this 'I know sis, it's impossible isn't it what shall I do?'

'That's up to you, do you think that you might go to the dinner dance?'

'I might.'

'What will you wear?'

'I've got the dress that I bought for the 'Ball' at the hospital.'

'A bit dressy for a dinner dance look if you really mean to go, I can lend you a dress, it's one that Dr Regan's wife gave to me when I was in service for them. It's a nice green velvet, it'll suit you. I don't want to encourage you though, don't let Mum know about it'

'Oh thanks Sis, what would I do without you?'

'Are you going to tell Mum that you're still going out with him.'

Just as it Was

'Not yet, I'll just tell her that it's a special dance at the hospital.'

'Well from what Mrs Regan used to say about the dinner dances I hope that you enjoy it, and if it gets that far I can't wait for the day that you bring this Dr home.' Babs looked at her sister with raised eyebrows. Julie sighed,

'Come on the kettle's boiling let's get the washing up done.'

Back on duty Julie was walking along the ground floor corridor towards the cloakroom.

'Nurse Spencer' she turned to see John hurrying towards her.

'Nice to see you back' he gave her a peck on the cheek and smiled broadly.

'John, I was going to put this note in the mailbox, I might as well give it to you now.'

'I hope that it says what I want it to say.'

'It says that I have arranged my off duty and that I would like to be your partner at the dinner.'

'I wasn't sure that you would come.'

'Well I'm a bit nervous about meeting your parents and I don't, I don't,' she looked at the floor not knowing how to continue.

'Go on.'

'I'm not sure about what this means John, perhaps I shouldn't say this but maybe you have plans that I don't know about.'

Just as it Was

Was she saying too much but meeting his parents seemed to be a pretty important step to her and she didn't want Dr Gibson to read too much into it.

'Julie, it's only a dinner dance, don't worry about it I'll pick you up shall I?'

'No don't do that, I'll get a taxi to the hotel, my parents don't know where I'm going and I think that it's better like that at the moment.'

He looked at her resignedly 'whatever you want to do, I'll be looking out for you about seven then, I'll meet you upstairs in the ballroom. I've got a few hours off tomorrow though, how about going out for a run with me, we could go through to Clumber Park, have a walk around the lake and a pot of tea somewhere.'

'John that would be lovely, I've got a half day so see you outside the nurses' home gate at two o.clock.

The day was bright and warm, as they motored along the Great North Road towards the park. It was refreshing to get away from the atmosphere of the hospital for a short while and as John drove a breeze playfully blew about their hair. Julie relaxed and was glad that she had agreed to a run out with him. He listened eagerly as she told him about her holiday in London.

'It seems to have made quite an impression on you.'

'London and the Rolands family were wonderful, they're typical cockneys warm hearted and welcoming and they made

Just as it Was

me feel really at home. Gran was a real character, I never had a Gran of my own my Grandparents were all dead before I was born.'

'Oh my family live to a ripe old age, I still have two Grandmothers and a Granddad. I don't see them often they live in Berkshire but when I was younger I spent a lot of time with them.' John smiled at his memories. "They had a lovely house in the countryside and my brother and I spent our holidays with them. Granddad took us boating and we visited all sorts of lovely places with them.'

'I've never been to Berkshire, I did spend holidays in the countryside though, my Uncle had a smallholding on the edge of Saddleworth Moor and as a family we sometimes went to stay for a week. I loved the moors and the old farmhouse, I never wanted to go back to Doncaster when I'd been there.'

John listened intently 'Have you been to Clumber Park before?'

'No I haven't John.'

'Well then, I think you're in for a nice surprise, we're almost there now.' True enough as they passed through the stone gateway Julie was delighted to see acres of trees and grassy areas unfold before her as John drove along the grey smooth path which led them to the car park. Smaller paths led off in all directions and she couldn't wait to see where they led to. 'Here let me put your jacket in the car boot, it's such a lovely day I don't think that you're going to need it.' As he helped her out of the coat Julie smiled up at him, it really was nice to be out with him again and she looked forward to their

Just as it Was

afternoon. 'Right what's it to be, a walk around the lake, a look at the church, or shall we make for the bridge and do a bit of bird spotting, I've brought the binoculars.'

'Anything you like John, lead the way.' There were few people about and as they took the path leading to the lake they walked hand in hand underneath a growth of sycamores where John threw his arm around Julie and kissed her cheek as she leaned towards him. 'I'm so glad that you could come today, it seems ages since we last went out and I wanted to see you again before the dance.'

'Why John is there something you want to tell me?'

'What makes you ask that?'

'I thought perhaps you might have had second thoughts about me meeting your parents.'

'No, not at all, you silly girl, why would I do that?'

'Because John, although I am very fond of you we are only friends and it does seem a big step to take.'

'You're afraid to meet them aren't you?'

'No, no I'm not, I just can't see why it's so important we're just friends.'

'Well that will have to be enough for now then, come on you faceless girl let's enjoy ourselves, I'll race you down to the lake.' As they reached the lake John took her hand and as they walked along the bank she exclaimed with pleasure and drew his attention every time that they came across something interesting, a growth of bulrushes in the water or a

Just as it Was

Coot diving into the water. They took it in turns to look through the binoculars at the Herons and other water fowl 'you're a real country lover aren't you?'

'What about you how do think of yourself, town or country?'

'A bit of each I think and I'll have to bear that in mind when I look for another post.'

'Are you leaving the hospital?'

'Probably next year I'll start looking for something more senior. I'd like a registrar's position somewhere, what about you what are you going to do when you're qualified?'

'I've over a year to go yet before my training's finished, I haven't thought much about it, I don't really want to just yet.'

'Oh well we'll have to wait and see, come on, if we hurry back to the cafe we'll be just in time for a pot of tea and a slice of their scrummy chocolate cake, before I have to get back to the hospital again.'

Just as it Was

20

Lectures and More Lectures

'Only a few more weeks on here and then I'll be on night duty again.' Julie and Nurse Foster were bathing the children and changing the babies nappies. 'Come on little fellow,' as she picked up the squiggling six month old baby Julie thought of Babs and the fact that she herself would soon be an Aunt. 'Just think, after all these years there'll be a baby in our family, this hands on experience'll come in useful.' Foster was just beginning to feed a tiny baby who was in for investigation, he was a prem and a poor feeder and she sighed as the baby fell asleep again as she tried to get him to suck. 'Well there's nothing like hands on experience but I'm not ready for babies yet, I've enjoyed it on here, but I want a bit of time for myself first, babies are sweet but they don't half take up some time.'

'Plenty of time for you, have you got a boy friend?'

Foster smiled, 'no time for a social life when the exams are due.' No Julie thought and after this dinner dance, I'll really have to get down to a bit of studying. Nursing isn't a job she told herself, it's a way of life. If I don't get my finals though it'll be a disaster. When the week of the dance arrived Julie was full of concern about it, why ever did I agree to go, she

Just as it Was

was uncertain about her feelings for John Gibson but he was a problem that she dismissed and refused to think about when she didn't see him. She had spent a lot of time studying recently and she had only been out with him one evening. I really like him she told herself, but he's going to leave next year if he gets another position, so things will sort themselves out. I will miss him but anyway him and me, no, it's just not possible. What about his parents then, what will you do about them she asked herself? and then she wondered again why on earth she had agreed to go to the dinner dance.

The ballroom was lit by splendid chandeliers which threw their glittering light over the well dressed people who had gathered for the occasion. Julie had dressed with the utmost care and she had made an appointment to have her usually wayward hair dressed in a sophisticated style. The green velvet dress which Babs had lent to her fitted over her slim youthful waist and accentuated the smooth curve of her hips as it dropped down to a length which was just above her golden sandals. She held a small gold coloured evening bag which Babs had also unearthed and a lightweight green velvet jacket completed her outfit. 'Julie, you look amazing,' John was waiting for her as she walked into the ballroom and he took her hand. 'Come and meet my parents, we're to join them on their table for dinner along with some of their friends. My brother and his girlfriend are here too, come and meet them.' Julie swallowed hard and she felt an urge to turn tail and run away, but with her hand in John's she followed him to where a group whom she recognised as his family were standing

Just as it Was

sipping their drinks. 'Mother Dad, this is Julie.' Mr Gibson smiled and stretched out his hand to grasp Julie's and he shook it warmly.' Mrs Gibson moved forward 'hello my dear, it's so nice of you to join us, there aren't many young people here so I hope that it wont be a dull evening for you.' Julie smiled back at the couple but she didn't know what to say, then John came to the rescue 'what would you like to drink Julie?'

'Oh just an orange juice please' she thought that she would need to be in full control of her senses tonight if she was going to get through, she hoped desperately that they were not going to ask her where she lived or what her family did. There were conversations going on all around from small groups about how their children were getting on at their public schools, and how well the markets were doing and what their latest car was. It was a world which Julie knew nothing about and she didn't see how she could talk to these people. She sipped her drink slowly and listened as John bantered with his brother David and others about their latest exploits. 'Excuse me John, I wont be a moment.' Julie had to escape she was absolutely dumb struck and she needed time to recover. She walked into the cloakroom and looked at herself in the mirror, the reflection of a figure came up behind her and she recognised David's girlfriend.

'Oh hello.'

'Are you O.K. Julie? John asked me to come and see if anything was wrong he was worried about you.'

Just as it Was

'Yes, yes, I'm fine thank you, I think the warmth of the room got to me a bit.'

'It is hot in there and these occasions are full of folks sounding off about their families and foreign holidays and such. There's a lot of hot air. If you're not used to that sort of thing it can be a bit overwhelming. John's parents are lovely people though, he talks about you very often Julie and they have really been looking forward to meeting you.' Julie looked at the other young woman she looked friendly enough but how far could she trust her, could she really confide in her how she felt. 'It really was the heat but I feel better now, I'm ready to go back in there.' The girls walked back towards the others who were still chatting together. As they approached John smiled at her anxiously, 'are you ready to eat Julie are you feeling alright?' she gathered herself and smiled back at him, she was going to make the most of this experience. After the first wave of uncertainty she told herself to pull herself together 'yes John I'm quite hungry as a matter of fact.' John looked relieved and took her hand as he led her over to the table where the waiters were preparing to serve the meal. Theirs was a large table seating a dozen or so people business colleagues of Mr Gibson and and also family members. John was on Julie's right and on her left was a man who looked to be in his late thirties probably, a very forthright person who was not afraid to express his views and make himself known. He turned to Julie, 'I'm Hugh Bedford, and this is my wife Angela,' Julie leaned forward and smiled at the woman who returned her smile. 'I take it you're the young lady whom John is always talking about.'

Just as it Was

John interrupted, 'yes this is Julie, we met at the hospital and tonight she's come along to meet all you lovely people and we're very much looking forward to enjoying ourselves, oh here comes the fish course, it looks very good.' Indeed the small portions of plaice, served in a shrimp sauce and garnished with parsley looked very appetising and as they ate pleasant conversation flowed around the table and Julie found herself relaxing into the atmosphere of the place. The rest of the meal lived up to the starter and as they made their way through the five courses and later listened to the speeches the company became more and more convivial. The sound levels increased and as the waitresses cleared the tables the company prepared for the dance as the orchestra took to the stage. 'I don't think I'll be able to dance after all that food,'

'We'll just sit for a little while then, come on let's find a quiet table somewhere, here we are, I want to get you to myself for a bit, you look so lovely Julie, I haven't had a chance to tell you yet.'

'Thank you John, and you look so very handsome in your dinner jacket, I'm enjoying myself the meal was very good. It's the first time that I've been to anything like this, a formal dance I mean,' Julie thought of the church hall and the dances at the pub where she had gone to dance after duty with her friends. The atmosphere here was champagne driven and the sophisticated crowd now relaxed after the dinner and the speeches, seemed part of another world.

'Well I'm glad that you're enjoying it it's a bit different isn't it; a bit more stuffy I suppose.'

Just as it Was

'Well they are the top brass of our town' she said chirpily. From a few yards away voices reached their ears. At a table which was hidden from theirs by an ornamental arrangement a group of people were talking and drinking. Although the words were spoken in an ordinary voice Julie heard the conversation clearly. 'She's a very pretty girl I can see why John would be attracted to her but I was talking to her as we having our meal and although she's bright and amusing she's quite unsophisticated I suppose you'd call her a breath of fresh air if you wanted to be kind.'

'What do you mean?'

'Well' er um, she certainly didn't go to a decent school, a grammar school I believe.'

'A grammar school; the speaker hesitated then 'oh! I see,' there was another pause 'but tell me what was the holiday like, did you enjoy St Moritz?'

The voice of Hugh Bedford and a colleague changed Julie's mood completely as she heard the words. From his expression John had heard the conversation and he rose from his chair angrily. 'Please John please, ignore it, don't make a fuss' she took hold of his sleeve.

'The man's a complete ass, who does he think he is.' Julie was convinced that the man's opinion was probably held by many others in the ballroom and she did feel as though she didn't belong there. She didn't want John to make a scene on her behalf. 'I think I'd like to dance John,' the orchestra had started up and the tune was one that she loved 'come on don't think anymore about it, I'm not upset.'

Just as it Was

'You are a remarkable girl Julie Spencer' he said as he pulled her gently out of the seat. As they reached the dance floor John took her in his arms and as the haunting tune of 'Down In The Glen' rang out from the small orchestra he rested his chin on her forehead and feeling the softness of her hair brush against him he was filled with tenderness towards her, he wanted to protect her and he drew her body closer.

'Though humble it may be, there an angel waits for me.' The words of the song as the vocalist sang into the microphone were currently popular with many. Julie softly sang them, almost to herself and as the lights were lowered in the ballroom to set the mood John said 'I'd love to take you away from all this, all these people, it would be wonderful to go somewhere where we can just be on our own, Scotland, North Yorkshire somewhere quiet and secluded just the two of us.' Julie felt a growing warmth towards him, was it the music and maybe the wine which they had insisted she drank with her meal. At the moment she thought I would love to do that how great it would be to jump into his precious little car and speed off to somewhere like the place in the song and be damned with everything and everybody, she rested her head dreamily on his shoulder.

'A penny for them' John said.

'I was just thinking how much I'm enjoying this dance, I love this song.' She lifted her arms putting them around his neck as they moved together slowly dancing to the music, other couples faded into the shadows and as John danced with her Julie was completely carried away by the moment and this

Just as it Was

feeling of oneness that was developing between them. Hang on though, reality crept in this just wouldn't do what on earth was she thinking of she must stop now. She removed her arms and pulled away from him. This place, these people, the lifestyle this was his world Hugh Bedford might be a pompous ass but he was right. It would never come to anything between her and John Gibson. She looked at him directly, ' John it's nice to dream but you're looking for a new post soon and. I've got to get ready for my finals.'

'When you get your finals you could come and find a position in a hospital close to me.'

'Oh John if only it was that simple, there are so many obstacles,' she drew close to him again, his presence winning her over he was such a lovely man. 'Let's just enjoy tonight and let the future take care of itself.'

Just as it Was

21

A Spell of Night Duty

The atmosphere was relaxed as the nurses chatted together in the comfortable armchairs of the sitting room. They were enjoying their two to four off duties and catching up with each other.

'I should be on night's but matron needs a senior nurse on days to cover for a couple of weeks and she's asked if I would do it.' Julie said.

'That's a reprieve, I hate night duty, I always feel half dead and I can't sleep for more than a few hours during the day, it's not normal.' Bessie Collins a large second year nurse was munching her way through a packet of salted crisps as she sat in the comfy armchair and revelling in the luxury of a couple of hours away from the tension of duties in the theatre. That morning had been particularly busy with Mr Warner's list including three meniscectomys (removal of a cartilage from the knee joint.) and two amputations, one minor and one above knee on a middle aged man whose gangrene had spread until the only option was to remove the limb. The orthopaedic surgeon could be irascible on occasions and this morning had been one of them. 'I wouldn't swap you, I don't like theatre, I like bedside nursing.' Julie picked up a copy of

Just as it Was

the nursing mirror and settled herself down to read the case history of a rheumatology patient.' The peaceful scene was disturbed as Chris Walker bounced into the room flopping into one of the spare chairs. 'I haven't seen you for ages Julie, I hear that you're going back to ward three.'

'I'm looking forward to it I'm only going for a short spell just to cover until the other senior nurse comes back, then I'm on there on night duty.'

'We had a bit of fun on there last week, you know the Rev comes round now and then and he brings and plays his music on that little organ, well Vera Sutton saw him in the ward ministering to one of the patients and as she went out of the ward to the office she saw the organ standing on the corridor. She's not too fond of organ music so seeing Nurse Morris who was just going back to the male ward Sutton beckoned her over and asked her to help to put the organ into the food lift and send it down onto the floor below. Morris is always up for a bit of fun so they quickly wheeled the organ away put it in the lift and dispatched it to ward two. 'Oh no,' the others were horrified and not a little amused. Nurse Walker continued after being doubled up with laughter. 'Then Morris nipped down the stairs and whipped it out onto the corridor then nipped back upstairs to find the Rev wandering about asking, 'has anyone seen my organ.' The nursing staff had been let in on what had happened and they were hysterical with laughter having to hide it and try to show concern when poor Rev Wright went round saying 'I'm sure I brought it up here with me.'

Just as it Was

'You rotten lot fancy doing that to a man of the cloth.' Julie said between her giggles.

'It was a bit of fun, that's all, we've got to let off steam sometime ' Christine replied.

It was nice to be back up there on ward three again and as she met up with Sister Robson and in the kitchen with Mrs Keogh, Julie remembered her times as a junior on that ward and the tales they had shared.

'Are you still wreaking havoc?'

Mrs Keogh, looked innocently at Julie, her big blue eyes laughing mischievously. 'What me, as if. We did have a queer how do you do up here a little while ago though, nothing to do with me'

'Oh yes.'

Father Wright lost his organ; you know the one 'ee plays 'is 'ymmns on 'ee were wandering all over lookin' forrit. Poor man, 'ee found it on ward two eventually, forgot where ee put it I suppose.' She burst into loud laughter, 'we all 'ave our own ideas about what 'appened, after all how can ye forget wheer you put yeer organ Nurse Spencer?'

'Mrs Keogh, you never change, and please don't' Julie said with a big smile on her face. All too soon her time relieving on ward three ended. The summer was swiftly drawing to a close and night duty loomed for Julie.

Just as it Was

'You'll have to hurry to catch the bus if you're to be on duty on time.' Eva Spencer looked up at the clock from the chair where she was sitting darning her husband's socks. The late September evening had darkened and the heavy cotton curtains had been drawn against the chilly night. Julie looked longingly at the cheerful hearth and wished that she didn't have to go out to catch the bus to the hospital. She would rather curl into a chair and read her book. She was enthralled with the story, Neville Shute's 'Requiem For a Wren' and she had neglected her studying and other activities as she had stolen time to read the book. 'I'm ready now Mum,' she bent down and kissed her Mum and went out into the chilly street. She was not looking forward to night duty, three months of utterly anti social life when she would wake up feeling gritty and venture out into the dark and then take up her duties as her fellow men slept.

The ward was busy, it was their urgency week, they had a few empty beds to take in those who were unfortunate enough to be taken ill suddenly or those who had come to grief by accident or other means. In a bed which was half way up the long Nightingale ward a heavy middle aged woman was breathing noisily. The nurses had settled the ward giving out the hot drinks and the medication and making sure that their patients were as comfortable as possible and most were well on their way to sleep. Mrs Ainsworth had been admitted the previous evening having swallowed some of the contents of a bottle of bleach. She was unconscious and struggling to breath and as Julie and Nurse Elliot carefully made her as comfortable as possible they were saddened at the tragedy of

Just as it Was

the poor woman's fate. Nothing could be done for her in the way of treatment all the nurses could do was to tend to her immediate needs. No one knew why or how she had come to swallow the bleach but the hopelessness of the matter cast a darkness over the ward, and a feeling of helplessness.

The houseman Dr Brentford had called in to check that there was nothing needed in the way of sedation or other care and now Julie and her junior were discussing the patients. 'Mr Edwards is going home tomorrow.'

'That'll be another bed available, we're a bit short at the moment, hope we don't get too much in the way of urgencies tonight.'

'You never know what it's going to be like, keep your fingers crossed.' There was a shout from down the ward 'nurse, nurse,' Julie hurried down to the caller, 'nurse can I have a bedpan please.'

Night Sister came onto the ward about half-past twelve and as she approached Mrs Ainsworth's bed she was greatly concerned. 'Are there no relatives to sit with this lady Nurse Spencer, she is gravely ill.'

'No Sister, there is no-one, we know very little about her, no one to call when the inevitable happens absolutely alone in the world as far as we know.'

'How sad, poor woman' night sister said as she gazed on the woman's tortured cyanosed face, (a bluish purely colour from lack of oxygen.) I think that it would be better if we put her in the side ward. I'll get the junior from ward two to sit

Just as it Was

with her, it's quiet on there so she can be spared. Mrs Ainsworth is going to die tonight nurse and we can't let her die alone.' The ward was disturbed as Julie and nurse Elliot with the help of the night porter moved the patient into the side ward, one or two of the other patients were awoken but the disturbance was kept to a minimum. Nurse Brown came up from ward two to sit by the dying woman's bed and as Julie walked out of the side ward she heard the phone ring. 'Can you get a bed prepared, we have to admit a patient with severe abdominal pain, possibly for theatre when the consultant has seen her.' It was the casualty officer from accident and emergency. What a night this is going to be, a real initiation, my first back on night duty, Julie thought.

As Julie wrote out the report Nurse Elliot collected the enamel bowls from the sluice and placed them on the patients' lockers. Soon the ward would become alive, it was five a.m. and as light from the dawning day began to creep in at the windows, the experiences of the night showed on the young nurses tired faces. Mrs Ainsworth had survived the night but only just. The patient who had been admitted had needed urgent surgery for the relief of a strangulated hernia and was now back on the ward with intravenous fluid being given together with aspirations through a nasal tube. As the urgent life saving procedures had been carried out with as little disturbance as possible to the other patients the doctors and nurses had accomplished their nights work. Soon medications would be given out, the backs rubbed, temperatures taken, toileting completed enemas given and at last when the day

Just as it Was

staff arrived Julie and Nurse Elliot would be able to go off duty and home to their beds.

'There's a letter for you.' Mrs Spencer was sorting out her sewing box and she looked up as Julie, after sleeping heavily during the day, came through to the living room for something to eat before she went back on night duty.

'Where is it.'

'On the dresser, I wonder who it's from?'

Julie picked up the letter and immediately recognised Colin's handwriting, the postmark was Doncaster, he must be home on leave.

'I'll look at it later, I haven't got time to read it now Mum.'

'Humph! I'll put the kettle on I've made you a sandwich, a nice bit of ham, if you fancy it.'

'Thanks Mum. I'll have to hurry though, I haven't got much time.'

As she took the report from day sister Julie was told that Mrs Ainsworth had died at ten oclock that morning.' 'She's out of her misery now, the poor woman hadn't a soul in the world as far as we know. How on earth she came to drink the bleach!' Sister gave a deep sigh.

'What happens then, who will sort her funeral out?'

Just as it Was

'The hospital almoner will deal with it and of course there'll be an inquest.'

'How do people come to be so alone in the world?'

'I don't know Nurse Spencer, perhaps we will never know.'

'Is there anything tucked away in the cupboard?'

Night Sister had done her round and the patients were all settled down. Julie and Nurse Jones from the male ward had slipped into the kitchen for their break. 'Nothing in here, lets ring Chester on ward two, see if she can send anything up in the food lift.' Julie picked up the kitchen phone and dialed ward two. 'Hi we're hungry, have you a bit of butter and Jardox going spare, the soup and cheese they sent up has all gone.'

'I can let you have a black clock sandwich if you like, that's all we've got in this kitchen tonight.'

Julie giggled, after last night the atmosphere was lighter and the time for a bit of fun overwhelmed the young nurses.

'The lift's on our floor, I'll send it down to you and you can send the sandwiches up.'

'Quick, slip into the office and get the bell that sister rings at the ward doors when it's time for visitors to leave. We'll put it on top of the food lift and send it down to Chester, it'll clang and scare 'em to death.'

Jones was soon back with the bell and the two managed to place it in the small space on top of the lift. Pressing the

Just as it Was

button they waited for the clanging, not a sound, the kitchen phone rang, 'hi your sandwiches are on the way up.' They waited as the sound of the lift coming up was heard and then a terrific crunching sound echoed through the kitchen.

Nurse Spencer and Nurse Jones looked alarmingly at one another. 'Oh my God, we've destroyed the food lift.'

'Quick press the button, see if it still works.'

The lift came down and the girls were horrified to see the bell handle broken and in bits. 'What have we done to Sister's bell, what shall we do?'

'Thank heavens the lift still works, we'll have to get rid of the bell.'

The kitchen door opened and Nurse Elliot from Julies ward came in.

'Nurse Spencer Mrs Wright can't sleep, oo'er what's happened to Sister Robson's bell?'

'We were having a bit of fun, it went wrong.'

'Looks like it, what are you going to do?'

'We'll have to get rid of it.'

'How are you going to do that.'

'Throw it in the river or something.'

'Give it to me, I live near the Don I'll get rid of it for you, when I was on days on here none of us liked going to stand at the door ringing the bell, it's nice to see the back of it.'

Just as it Was

'You wonderful girl', Julie couldn't believe the other girl's reaction, 'and please not a word to anyone.'

'I promise, just wrap it up and I'll put it in my bag, I wonder what Sister Robson's going to say though when she comes to miss it.'

Back on the ward Julie approached Mrs Wright. 'What's the problem Mrs Wright, why can't you sleep?'

'I'm going home tomorrow nurse and I don't know 'ow I'm going to manage.'

'Why, what are you worried about?'

'I don't know 'ose going to do the cooking and the cleaning, me 'usbands on nights and I've got three young children.'

'Haven't you anyone who might help, friends or family?'

'No nurse, we've not lived here long, and me family 'ave problems of their own.'

'I'll have a word with Sister Robson in the morning, perhaps some help can be arranged. Would you like a cup of milk to help you to sleep?'

'Ooh thanks nurse, that would be nice, I'm sorry to be a nuisance.'

It was a fact that there was little communication between the community and the hospital and Julie wondered if help could be arranged for Mrs Wright. She would do what she could anyway. The poor woman had her breast removed and going home to her full responsibility of caring for home and family, would be a challenging task. Now that the ward was quiet

Just as it Was

Julie had the chance to take out Colin's letter. What did he have to say it was more than eighteen months since she had heard from him.

Dear Julie.

You will be surprised to hear from me after all this time, and although I have often thought about writing to you before the fact that you may not want to hear from me put me off. I miss you so much though that I have at last decided that I must do it to see if there is any chance of us getting back together.

I wont pretend that I haven't seen anyone else because I have, I have been out with quite a few girls but I never felt the same for them as I felt for you. I expect that you will have had other boyfriends too and if there is someone special then I am sorry and I don't want to spoil things for you. I will be out of the army in a few months time and although I still think of going to Canada if we were to get back together it would be what you want to do.

It was such a silly way that we fell out, we were such a long way from each other which didn't help and both of us so wrapped up in our careers. I do hope that you will write back and let me know how things are. I still love you.

                              Colin.

Julie folded the letter and put it in the pocket of her uniform dress. What could she say, what was she going to do.

Just as it Was

22

Goodbye

As she opened the door to Babs Julie was amazed by the appearance of her sister. 'Crikey, don't tell me it's twins.'

'Ooh, let me inside, the wind blows down this street like a knife.' True since Julie had finished her stint of night duty the weather had tumbled into a grey cold and wet late Autumn. None of the brilliant sunshine and bronze colours which usually graced the season and now Babs wanted to escape into the warmth of the fireside.

'So, you're back in the land of the living?'

'Yes, almost, I'm sorry I haven't seen much of you but with studying and being on nights I haven't seen much of anyone.'

'Where's Mam?'

'She's out with Sherry, gone up to the shops while she's out, needs some more dog biscuits I think. What about you are you back on drinking tea yet, shall I put the kettle on?'

'I'd love a cup, I've only a couple of months to go now you know and I've an appetite like a horse.' Julie laughed,

'I'm sorry to hear that sis, I was going to offer you a piece of Mum's caraway seed cake but I better get you a bag of hay.'

Just as it Was

'Ha, ha, a piece of cake will be lovely.' Babs shook her head at her sister and went to the kitchen cupboard to take out the cups and saucers as Julie put the kettle on the gas ring. 'So how are you getting on?'

'How do you mean, I'm working hard, I'm not very well off, and I've got my finals coming up in a few months time.'

'And what about the handsome young doctor?'

Julie hadn't expected this, Babs was still the only one in the family who knew of her ongoing friendship with John Gibson, and she was unsure how to answer.'

'Babs I don't have time for romance, I see him now and again and I enjoy myself when I'm with him but it doesn't go further than that.'

'I suppose that's O.K. then, does he feel the same?'

Julie looked at her sister and sighed, 'no he's more serious.'

'Great, what are you going to do?'

'What can I do. I can't bring him home, look at the furniture, the little settee the washing airing off, hanging here in the living room all week, how could I bring him to our house. Not only that what would he talk to Dad about, what could he talk to any of us about. We've nothing in common.'

'Have you been to his home?'

'I've been invited but I'm not going, I have no intention of becoming seriously involved with him.'

'Then tell the poor chap, you're not being fair to him, why don't you tell him?'

Just as it Was

'To tell you the truth sis I really like him, in fact I think I'm a little bit in love with him.'

'You can't be a little bit in love, there's no such thing, you thought that you were a little bit in love with Colin didn't you?'

'I've heard from Colin he's almost finished his National Service, he wants us to meet up again.'

'Well you've got some decisions to make haven't you? you better make your mind up.' The front door opened and Sherry came bounding into the room wagging her tail and nuzzling up to Babs. Mrs Spencer looked at her daughters, 'now then what have you two been talking about?'

'Oh just this and that Mam, catching up with things' they replied.

'You know she's heard from Colin again.'

'She's just been telling me.'

'Nice lad Colin and you've not written back yet have you?'

'No Mum but I will do soon, I've a few things to sort out first.'

'You've a few letters to write, what about writing back to your friend in London, Jane Rolands she wrote to you two weeks ago.'

'How is she?' Babs had heard about the visit and showed great concern for Jane.

'She's fantastic and she manages to work and the boy who she met when I was over there has kept in touch with her and she's seeing him quite regularly.'

Just as it Was

'That's wonderful, do you think that you might go over there again?'

'Who knows, who knows what the future holds.' Julie replied.

She was working on days on women's surgical now. Although not in the uniform she was taking on many of the duties of Staff Nurse and she worked well with Sister Robson. This lady still lamented the disappearance of her hand bell but that object was well and truly sitting in the depths of the River Don and those concerned kept the secret to themselves.

Occasionally Julie met John on the corridors or in outpatients and at this moment he was heading towards her looking quite serious. 'Julie, where have you been , I haven't seen you for ages.'

'I know John, I've been on nights and I've been studying.'

'I thought that you might have been at the dance in the Badminton Hall, I went there especially to see you, I don't have a phone number I never know where you are, how can I keep in touch with you?'

'You see John, that's the difference between you and me, I don't have a phone, I don't have the many things that you have. There's no way that we can keep on seeing each other, our lives are so different.'

'What are you saying Julie?'

Just as it Was

'I'm saying John that I'm not going to see you again, I am so sorry but I can't just be friends any longer and we can never be more than that.'

John looked astounded, 'but Julie, you can't, you can't just walk away, I know that you have feelings for me.'

'I don't Deny it John, but I'm not going to see you again.' She reached up and kissed him on the cheek, before she let the tears fall, she gave him a quick hug turned away hurriedly and walked away back up to her ward leaving him standing on the corridor watching her disappear from his life.

Just as it Was

23

Outpatients

'What is wrong with you Julie, you're like a cat with the mange.' Vera Sutton looked at her friend over her coffee cup. The busy cafe buzzed with the sound of the machines and from the juke box Jonny Ray was singing, 'Cry'. Groups of young people were laughing and joking with each other as they took time to get together on this Saturday morning. Some of them would later be going on to the local game to watch the Rovers play at Belle Vue while Vera and Julie would be going back on duty at the hospital after their morning off .

'I'm O.K. Julie picked up her cup and drained the last dregs of coffee from it, there's quite a lot happening at the moment and I'm a bit tired that's all.'

'Well buck yourself up, you've been moping around for weeks now, I thought you were ill or something.'

'It's nice of you to be concerned Vera but really I'm fine, don't worry.'

Since breaking off her friendship with John Gibson Julie had felt forlorn and apathetic. She had met him once since then, a chance meeting as she was going to the dining room and he

Just as it Was

stopped her and told her that he had applied for a post of registrar at a hospital in Devon. They had parted awkwardly and now if she saw him in the distance she went out of her way to avoid him but she thought of him constantly although she knew that she had made the right decision.

After a routine day, Julie was not looking forward to Saturday evening. This was always bed changing day and as the nurses worked their way down the long lines of beds on each side of the ward throwing the soiled sheets and pillowcases into the used linen trolley they chatted to the patients, rubbed their backs and skipped backwards and forwards to the linen room for clean sheets and pillowcases. It seemed an endless and dreary task for Saturday night when other young women were putting on their make up and pretty dresses and going out to the Coop dance hall or the St Jame's Baths to dance the night away. Julie would be glad when she went off duty and she felt an overwhelming tiredness swamp her.

Pull yourself together Julie, I don't know what's the matter with you lately, I haven't seen you smile for weeks, what's wrong?'

'Nothings wrong Mum, I'm just tired, I can't help it.'

'Well pull yourself together, we've the baby to look forward to you'll be an Auntie soon and Christmas is coming before long.' She gathered up her dusters 'did you ever write back to Colin, he'll be out of the army soon.' Mrs Spencer was polishing the

Just as it Was

sideboard, dressed in her old cardigan with her pinafore fastened around her body and a scarf tied turban wise on her head Julie looked at her. This is Mum's life she thought; working from dawn 'til dusk keeping our home clean and polished, shopping cooking the meals and scraping the money together to pay the bills. I can't remember when she last had a holiday. What will my life be like in twenty years time will I be doing the same? She shook herself, her life had changed so much since she went into nursing. The people that she had met were from all walks of life. Not only her colleagues but patients who came from so many different backgrounds. People like Doreen Stapleton with whom she'd got on so well. London and the Rowlands family. So many doors had been opened to her. The outings that she had taken with John in his car. Clumber Park was almost on the doorstep but if she hadn't been taken there in his car who knows whether she would even be aware of its existence. True Conisborough Castle and Hexthorpe Flatts were more easily accessed but anything outside the five mile radius boundary was a rare journey. Well she thought it's up to you if you don't get on and pass your state finals you probably will end up being like your Mum, and what about Colin how about replying to his letter, he deserves a reply. 'I'm going upstairs Mum I'm going to do some studying and I'll write the letter to Colin.'

'And as you're going take this washing upstairs and put it in the airing cupboard. Let's have this place tidy for the weekend' her mother replied.

The bedroom which she had shared with Doris was cold and uninviting but her parents had given Julie a little table and

Just as it Was

and a one bar electric fire so that she could study away from the noise of the rest of the family and the radio. Taking out her books she opened them and decided today to read up the inner workings of the respiratory system. She might get a question on any of the systems and she would have to work her way through them all. After an hour or so she had done enough about the bronchii and the pulmonary arteries and she sat gazing into space. She thought about Colin and the fact that she still owed him a reply to his letter so taking out her writing case she began.

Dear Colin.

It was nice to hear from you and I am sorry that I have taken so long in replying to your letter. It would be nice to meet up again although I don't have a lot of time to spare with the exams coming up early next year. Perhaps we can go to the cinema or something. You told me that you had been out with a few different girls since we fell out. Well I haven't had anyone special but I have been going out with someone but I'm not seeing him any more. I went to London in the summer to stay with a friend and her family and I really enjoyed it. I wouldn't mind going back there again. Do you still want to go Canada? Babs expects a baby in another month or so and we are all excited about that and the rest of the family are all well.

I must stop and get on with my revision Colin. Let me know when you will be home.

Julie.

Just as it Was

As she pushed the dressing trolley back into the sluice Nurse Elliot approached Julie. 'Matron's in the office, she wants to see you.'

'Wants to see me, what have I done wrong?' Miss Ferguson was renowned for dressing down her nurses very pleasantly to start with. Her manner initially lulled them into a false confidence but then she began to prevaricate and she often ended up in a fury sending the poor offender shaking like a leaf as she sped away as fast as possible. I've done nothing wrong, whatever can it be? Julie dumped the trolley intending to clear it later and making for Sisters office she knocked on the door. 'Come in.' The two senior members of staff were sitting at the desk and as Julie went in Miss Ferguson beamed at her. 'Ah Nurse Spencer, it's nice to see you, how are you getting on up here?' So, did this bode well, Julie hoped so.

'I like it Matron, I like it very much I'm used to this ward'

'Yes, that may well be nurse but you have spent a long time on surgical wards and we are short of a nurse in outpatients. I would like you to move to that department.'

'I hope that Sister Robson has been pleased with me Matron.'

'Of course I have, you have helped out magnificently you have spent a lot of time on surgery and it was useful to have someone who knew the running of the ward.'

'It's nothing to do with that nothing at all to do with how you've carried out your duties; staff nurse is ready to come back on here, so next week you will be working in outpatients.' Matron smiled again, it will be good experience

Just as it Was

for you, your training needs to cover all aspects of nursing, thank you nurse, you can go back to the ward now.'

As she dismantled her trolley and washed the stainless steel bowls and forceps before putting them in the steriliser Julie pondered on the fact that she would be working in outpatients. Well that wasn't too bad she thought and I'll be working with Chris Walker. It'll be nice to work with Chris again.

It was the paediatric clinic today. The seats outside Dr Horrocks clinic were full of Mums and their little ones waiting to be seen. Julie called in Mrs Parker with her young child a slightly built fair haired little lad who didn't look very happy to be there. She smiled at the mother and held out her hand to the little boy 'come on your Mum's coming with you we've got some nice pictures to show you.' The clinic was as child friendly as it could be with a few children's books and one or two pictures and toys to distract the younger patients.

The doctor examined the little boy thoughtfully. 'How often does he have the fits Mum?' he asked the anxious mother.

'He's had two or three doctor mostly when he's off colour.'

'Over what period of time?'

'The first one was when he was about three and the last one was on his birthday last week, he was four last week.'

'And was there anything else, did he have a temperature, any signs of a cough or a rash?'

Just as it Was

Julie listened interestedly as the doctor took the childs history. Dr Horrocks had come from one of the London Hospitals and he was well known for his work with children she found the work very different from her previous nursing, mostly of adults and she felt that she was crossing new boundaries. It was a challenge to put the children in as friendly and ordinary atmosphere as possible while paying attention to the professional aspect as well. The next patient was a small baby and he had been referred because of failure to gain weight. Dr Horrocks asked the mother to carefully tell him how much milk the baby took and how often she fed him, he turned to Julie. 'Nurse will you weigh the baby and work out what his feeds should be?' Julie hadn't a clue and thought that she better own up immediately. Dr Horrocks looked at her in surprise then he smiled, 'two and a half ounces per pound bodyweight divided by the number of feeds nurse.' Picking up the baby and walking over to the table where the scales were she took the piece of paper that the doctor had passed to her and hoped that her maths would stretch to the task. The mother looked on interestedly,' I'm glad that you didn't ask me to do that doctor' she said and the atmosphere was relaxed instantly as they all smiled. The clinic was busy and as others came along to have bloods taken Julie was kept fully stretched all afternoon. She had been working in outpatients now for about three weeks and this afternoon the last patient had been seen as Dr Horrocks gathered up his papers into his briefcase. As had become his habit the consultant spoke to her about the cases that they had seen. He was speaking to her about baby clinics out in the community where babies were seen regularly and an eye was kept on their development. He looked at her intently,are you enjoying working in outpatients with the children Nurse Spencer I realise that it is different for you?'

'I am I wasn't too sure at first about working with children especially babies, but I've really found it very interesting.'

'Yes I see that, you get on very well with the children and the parents I hope that you'll be able to work in this clinic for a while longer. Have you ever thought about doing your children's training?'

'Well no, I haven't decided what I'm going to do when I get my finals, if I get my finals,' she added 'where would I go to train?'

'The Childrens Hospital, Great Ormond St, I know it well.'

'You mean go to London, would I have a chance of getting in there?'

'I'm sure that you would and anyway, I would be pleased to put in a word for you.'

'Dr Horrocks it's something that I've never considered you've set me thinking now, I've never thought seriously about what I should do next but I have been to London and I enjoyed it very much. It would be wonderful to work there the work in this clinic's been so interesting, I like the idea. Thank you I'll talk to my family about it.'

As Julie took the files back to the records office, she pondered on the idea put to her by the paediatrician, it would be a completely new life experience, out of Yorkshire, into the metropolis. What about the other nurses on the course, they wouldn't be Yorkshire girls, not like her friends Vera and Christine and the others. Perhaps it's time that I stretched my wings a bit, she smiled as she handed the records over to Mr Dawson who was in charge of the office. 'Had a good clinic today Nurse Spencer?'

'Very good Mr Dawson, yes I think that it's been very good indeed.'

Just as it Was

24

Re-union

Julie kept one eye on the weather as the angry sky threatened those who were hurriedly nipping in and out of the shops on the High Street trying to complete their Christmas shopping. It was her day off and as she searched for a present for her newly born niece she reflected on past events. I've got to hurry, mustn't be late I've promised to meet Colin. Her life had taken a turn which she never would have envisaged twelve month ago. As she had nervously picked up the papers in the silent atmosphere of the Badminton Hall last October she had turned them over with trepidation her future depended on passing the state registration exam. She remembered the feeling she had on receiving the results, her stomach had done a somersault as she picked up the envelope but relief flooded through her as she read that she had been successful and that she was now on the register at last a State Registered Nurse. Her commitment to revision and her determination had stood her in good stead. The work in the paediatric clinic had opened up a new future to her and was now paying dividends. Dr Horrocks had been true to his word and after applying to Great Ormond Street Hospital she had an interview in the New Year. How much it had been due to his influence she didn't know but Julie was delighted with

Just as it Was

the prospect of living and working in London. Jane had written to her, she and Duncan were seeing each other regularly now and Julie felt that it wouldn't be long before they were announcing their engagement. If she was successful in gaining a place at the hospital she could take up her friendship with the Rowlands family again, Gran and Jane and her parents had often been in her thoughts, she had a ready made family there. 'I'll need it Julie thought, but hey, I've got to get through the interview first I wonder what that'll be like. She looked at her watch, she had promised to meet Colin in Priestnalls at one oclock, she had better hurry or she would be late.

He was sitting alone at a table looking thoughtful with a cup of steaming coffe in his hands as she arrived. 'Sorry I'm a bit late, the Christmas shopping slowed me down.'

'Don't worry, I've not been here long, what are you going to have?'

'Ooh, beans on toast and a pot of tea I think, what about you?'

'Same, I'll have the same as you.' They ordered the food and Julie undid the buttons on her coat. The temperature in the cafe was at odds with that in the wintery streets and as she looked around she wondered how much longer she would be here in Doncaster coming to these familiar places. 'I enjoyed myself last night Julie' there was a distance between them the separation had altered the easy way that had existed when they first met. 'Yes, so did I.'

'Thank you for seeing me again, I didn't know if you would.'

Just as it Was

'Why did you think that?'

'I thought that you had someone else.'

'There is no-one Colin.'

'Perhaps there's a chance for me then?'

'I don't think I'm ready for a serious relationship, if I get into Great Ormond Street I'm going to be in London for at least a couple of years. Julie had made her decision and now was the time to let Colin know. Perhaps I shouldn't have seen him again she thought but what's done is done. She had been curious to see how she would feel and now she knew, knew what she wanted. 'What about your plans, now that you're out of the army what are you going to do?'

'I haven't decided yet my old jobs available if I want it.'

'What were you doing in Richmond, why didn't you come back to Doncaster when you finished your service in the army?'

'Oh I made friends up there, and there was a job going, Richmond's a lovely place but the job came to an end so I decided to come back home.'

'What will you do now?'

'I don't know Julie, it depends on you I suppose.'

'I can't make any promises about my future Colin, if I get in at Great Ormond Street, I'll be away from Doncaster for a long time.'

'I could come to London to visit you.'

Just as it Was

Please, let's wait and see, I don't think that either of us is in a position to make decisions at the moment.' They slowly ate their meal as the noise of conversation and the music made it almost impossible for them to talk. After finishing the meal Colin paid the bill and Julie picked up her parcels as they left the coffee bar, and made their way into the street.

'I'll wait for you, you know, I'll wait for you Julie, we should never have fallen out.'

She smiled at him,'You don't have to you know, we were very young Colin, we still are. Things have changed, we've changed let's wait and see. Come on we'll catch the bus and get off home.'

'Can I meet you from the hospital tomorrow, we can still be friends can't we?'

'Not tomorrow Colin but we'll make some plans for over Christmas if you like, no strings though.'

'No strings.'

The appointment for Julies interview was arranged for mid-January. Her parents were to accompany her to London. It was not often they went away and with Mr Spencer's privilege tickets as a bonus for working for the L.N.E.R. it made the trip more affordable and they looked forward to the day out. Walking out of Kings Cross Station London looked grey and forbidding. The noise and the busy roads and the numbers of people all looking purposeful and remote made Julie and her

Just as it Was

parents feel uncomfortable and out of their depth. 'I think this is where we catch the bus to the hospital.'

'It's not like Doncaster is it?' Mrs Spencer was beginning to feel that she would rather be anywhere other than here. The unfamiliar streets and the noise were as foreign to her as laughter in a library and she felt daunted and ill at ease. 'Come on, they're only people like us, here comes our bus.' Mr Spencer was asserting himself, after all he had fought in the trenches for his country and travelled to many places with the army and he was full of pride to be in the capital it was his capital today. The ride to the hospital took about fifteen minutes and as they climbed from the bus and stood in front of the building where Julie was to have her interview it was her turn to feel intimidated. The large building with it's many windows loomed before her inhospitably, to her it felt strange and impenetrable, she took a deep breath. 'Come on, let's find the entrance.' Mr Spencer drew himself up and his wife and daughter followed on. Entering the building they were shown to a corridor where they were to wait for the interview to be given. After a short while a woman dressed in a tweed skirt and a very warm looking jumper showed Julie into an office where matron was waiting for her. 'Good afternoon Miss Spencer, I do hope that you had a good journey and found us easily enough.'

Julie looked at her and smiled, she was feeling nervous but doing her best to hide it. 'Yes Matron we had a good journey thank you.'

'Have you been to London before?'

Just as it Was

'I have, I had a short holiday here recently but I'm not all that familiar with it.'

'And how do you think that you will feel, being so far away from your family?'

'I am very close to my family, and I suppose that I will miss them at first but there is a good rail link between my home town and London and I do have friends in London who I stayed with during my holiday.'

'Good' Matron smiled 'and what hobbies do you have, do you read go to the theatre play tennis?'

'I like to read, when I get the time and I occasionally visit the theatre. It's mostly local productions, I have to go to Sheffield if I want to see the professional companies.' Julie felt that she was coping pretty well so far but these really weren't the questions that she had been expecting. 'And what do you read?' Matron asked, Julie was beginning to relax now.

'I like to read Thomas Hardy and the Brontes, I like the classics and I like to read topical magazines, we take the Illustrated every week and it keeps me in touch with things that are happening now. I go to the cinema too I saw Red Shoes recently, with Moira Shearer taking a wonderful part I like ballet and music.'

'I see that's good, and what about being in a strange city with people that you don't know, will you find that difficult?'

'I want to do my children's training and I'm prepared to do all it takes in order to do that.' The probing questions continued, she's trying to find out if I'm the right calibre, Julie thought.

Just as it Was

After more conversation which she managed to take on board comfortably matron stood up. 'Well now come along nurse, I'll show you some of the wards.' They walked a short distance before reaching several small single cubicles. 'These are where our patients are nursed and the children each have a special nurse allocated to them. We do have four bedded wards as well. These are where you would eventually be working.'

Julie looked and thought of the children's wards in the hospital at home. In comparison these wards were sterile and shut off, the open ward she was used to contained both cots and beds and there was a friendliness which was warming and contagious. 'You will realise nurse that we deal with specialist cases here and the need for one to one nursing is often necessary.'

'Yes matron, it is very different from the children's wards I have worked on before but I can see that it is necessary in a hospital like this to have this sort of accommodation.'

'Indeed, you would find many things different but I realise that you are keen to join us,' she looked directly at Julie 'I think that it can be arranged ' Julie was elated.

'Thank you matron I will do my very best. I am looking forward to fitting in and doing my childrens' training here, I want to be a good children's nurse' she was filled with excitement and couldn't wait to get out and tell her parents.' I will send out the relevant details to you in the post nurse, and I look forward to you becoming one of our nurses. You will of course need accommodation and I will let you have

Just as it Was

details of that.' Matron held out her hand, it has been pleasant meeting you, we have had quite a number of nurses coming from Yorkshire who trained here.'

'Oh, perhaps I will meet some of them, thank you matron.' Julie took the hand which was offered and after shaking it warmly she bid matron goodbye. Her parents were waiting for her and as they saw their daughter approach them they could tell that the news was going to be positive. This was it then their youngest daughter was to move to London to one of the best hospitals in the world. Their pride was tinged with regret, the family would now be split Julie would be the first to move out of her home town and the closely knit family would be depleted but they would cope, they were pleased that their daughter had achieved a place at this prestigious hospital and if that was what she wanted they hoped that her career in nursing would lead to even greater things.

'Come on then, let's celebrate I expect we'll be making quite a few visits to London Mam' Julie's father took his wife's arm as she sniffed, rather disapprovingly Julie thought.

'It's not like Yorkshire.' Mrs Spencer looked around her at the madding crowds and the smoggy atmosphere. 'No love it's not, but never mind, let's celebrate anyway let's go and have a meal in Lyon's Cafe.' Dad led the way out of the hospital followed by Julie and her Mum through the lofty streets of the capital.